—DETOUR—
UTAH

—DETOUR—
UTAH

MYSTERIES, LEGENDS AND PECULIAR PLACES

LYNN ARAVE & RAY BOREN

Published by The History Press
Charleston, SC
www.historypress.com

Front cover, clockwise from top left: Pecked and painted birds and animals, and more mysterious shapes, decorate Utah's Nine Mile Canyon. Balanced Rock poses precariously in Arches National Park. The Moki Dugway, a notorious but popular unpaved road, drops off Cedar Mesa. Southeastern Utah's Navajo Mountain rises beyond Lake Powell on the Colorado River. *Ray Boren photos. Back cover, top*: Venice Carson Flygare poses in front of Devil's Slide in 1947, when the highway ran right next to it in the pre-freeway era. *Flygare-Arave family photo. Back cover, bottom*: Landscape artist Robert Smithson's famed *Spiral Jetty* unfurls into Great Salt Lake's red-tinted waters. *Ray Boren photo.*

First published 2021

ISBN 9781540247551

Library of Congress Control Number: 2021931098

Notice: The information in this book is true and complete to the best of our knowledge. It is offered without guarantee on the part of the authors or The History Press. The authors and The History Press disclaim all liability in connection with the use of this book.

To our late parents, for cultivating our yen to wonder about and explore Utah's highest highs, lowest lows and everything in between.

CONTENTS

Acknowledgements   9
Introduction   11

PART I. MYSTERIOUS PLACES
1. Navajo Mountain: Sacred—and Remote   15
2. Rainbow Bridge: "Lore" and "Found"   20
3. Noah's Ark: In Southern Utah?   25
4. Nine Mile Canyon: Art Gallery in Stone   28
5. The Pando Clone: Many from One   33
6. Chinatown: Red Rock in Northern Utah   36
7. Peter Sinks: Hyper-Cold Dip   40

PART II. LEGENDS OF UTAH'S PAST
8. A Real Howard Stark: He Died in Utah   47
9. Layton's Snow Horse: Pioneer Landmark   50
10. Ben Lomond: Mountain of Dreams   53
11. Old Ephraim: Legendary Grizzly   57
12. Levan, Utah: No Navel Here!   61
13. Oak City: Almost Atomic City?   65
14. Kanab Rocks: Too "Bright" for Hollywood   68

PART III. UTAH HIGHS AND LOWS
15. South Kings Peak: Not Utah's Highest   73

CONTENTS

16. Mount Nebo: Wasatch Exclamation Point!   78
17. La Sal Mountains: Balcony of the Beehive State   84
18. Beehive Peak: A Red Pyramid   89
19. Notch Peak: Acrophobic Nightmare   93
20. Beaver Dam Wash: Utah's Basement   97

PART IV. UTAH HEAVEN AND HELL
21. Zion Canyon: In Heaven's Name   103
22. Cathedral Valley: Temples of the Sun and Moon   108
23. The Great Stone Face: Religious Icon   113
24. Monte Cristo: Utah's Mountain of Christ   116
25. Devil's Gate: Pioneer Bugaboo   119
26. Devil's Slide: Wicked Chute   125
27. Gog and Magog: Twin Rugged Peaks   130

PART V. FORGOTTEN PLACES
28. Fremont Island: Grave Robber to Phantom Coyote   137
29. Malan Heights: Copacabana of the West   142
30. Weber Power Plant: Marvel of Its Time   147
31. Lake Park: Prequel to Lagoon   150
32. This Is the Place: The Original   154
33. Fingers of the Kolob: Unheralded Zion View   158

PART VI. MAN-MADE WONDERS
34. Moki Dugway: "Chill Factor" Cliff Driving   163
35. Zion Tunnel: Drilled from the Middle   168
36. U-143: Steepest State Road in Utah   173
37. Duchesne Tunnel: Through the Uintas   175
38. Granite Vaults: Arsenal of Genealogy   180
39. Kennecott Mine: The Missing Mountain   184
40. Kennecott Smokestack: Reaching for the Sky   188
41. Francis Peak: Lofty Outpost of Domes   193
42. *Spiral Jetty*: Art with a Salty Twist   198

Bibliography   203
About the Authors   207

ACKNOWLEDGEMENTS

his book chronicles a few of the outdoor "adventures" of Lynn Arave and Ray Boren in Utah. At times, they were accompanied by their friend Ravell Call, whose companionship and skills were invaluable and much appreciated. Most of the treks took place between 1990 and 2012, but several are more recent. All three men worked for the *Deseret News*, Utah's first newspaper. Arave was a reporter, Boren a reporter and editor and Call a photographer.

Sharing both a bear-went-over-the-mountain curiosity and a certain sense of adventure, Arave and Boren often hiked and explored together. But they were just as likely to wander off by themselves or with other companions, as the case may be. Arave, for example, hiked to northern Utah's Peter Sinks on multiple occasions, first with a brother, Wayne Arave, and later with a friend, Scott Steele, and more recently with a television news crew. A son, Roger Arave, accompanied Lynn Arave to South Kings Peak, Gog and Magog, Notch Peak (with Boren) and the Great Stoneface. A friend, Dave Jenkins, biked and hiked with Lynn to Chinatown. Another son, Taylor Arave, hiked with him to the original Lake Park site, to Fremont Island and to Malan's Basin, all chronicled here. For his part, Boren visited Nine Mile Canyon and the Pando Aspen Clone on his own and occasionally with friends. In some instances, Boren and Lynn Arave traveled to certain locales at different times, providing information and photos to this project. Boren also took thousands and thousands of photographs all over Utah.

Acknowledgements

A majority of the photographs in the book and most of those on the cover were taken by the authors, Ray Boren and Lynn Arave. Roger Arave, Liz Arave Hafen and LeAnn Arave also contributed photos. Vintage images were provided by the Utah State Historical Society and Utah's Division of State History.

Credit also goes to the *Deseret News* for initially publishing reports about some treks. Arave, Boren and Call generally would visit locations and then write about what they saw and did. Often the reportorial result was a hybrid of personal time mixed with work time.

Some credit also goes to the *Ogden Standard-Examiner*. Arave wrote a page-one weekly history column for that newspaper for about eighteen months after he retired from the *Deseret News*. Some of those stories, in part, are in this book. He followed that stint with a monthly history column in the *Deseret News*, and again, portions of that writing are included here. In most cases, the predecessor newspaper stories have been updated and revised for presentation in the book.

Credit is also due to Utah digitalnewspapers.org and newspapers.com, where histories of subjects in this book have been enhanced through keyword searches, not possible until recent years.

We hope readers of this book will appreciate the intriguing yet sometimes obscure landscapes and features of Utah we've selected to showcase.

INTRODUCTION

Curiosity, the old proverb warns, killed the cat.
　　Yet inquisitiveness is the essence of the book before you. We're always wondering: What is on top of that mountain and what is on the other side? Where is that? How did this happen? What is around the next bend? Perhaps that helps explain why we have reconnoitered so many obscure and unusual places in Utah, the Beehive State, as well as researched and written about them, trying to share what we saw and found out. It is all about the "quest."

From the highlight of finding, measuring by GPS and reporting the geographic lowest elevation in Utah in 2006 (now the state's standard number for the low point) to getting to the top of Navajo Mountain (an almost forbidden place for outsiders) to confirming that Ben Lomond is indeed the mountain that inspired the Paramount Motion Pictures logo, occasionally these "adventures" actually helped make a wee bit of history, instead of just serving as trips to report about it.

Utah is a landscape of wide-open spaces and boasts some of the most impressive peaks in the lower forty-eight states. In fact, if you combine the highest elevations in each of Utah's twenty-nine counties, the average elevation for Utah is actually higher than any of the other forty-nine states, including Alaska and Colorado, though admittedly none of its peaks match their highest of the high.

Hiking and exploring has been invigorating and enlightening. But it is also worth emphasizing that the Utah outdoors can be dangerous. With sudden weather changes, heat and cold, lightning and hail, rough terrain and dizzying cliffs, it pays to use common sense and special care when trekking Utah. Some places might not be safe to travel to in winter, given exposure or avalanche hazards. Others might be inhospitable in late spring, summer or early fall, with scorching temperatures, limited water sources and flash-flood potential. Attention and respect also should be paid when visiting areas where there is private property or restricted access.

Note that because of the passage of time, some of those quoted as sources in this book might have changed jobs in the years. Nevertheless, their comments and historical references likely still hold true.

Original newspaper publication dates, if pertinent, are listed in the bibliography. Most of the topics have been expanded on since such publication.

If you would like to learn about even more Utah history, consider visiting Lynn Arave's blog, *The Mystery of Utah History*, at https://mysteryofutahhistory.blogspot.com.

We hope you are primed for a bit of armchair exploration. Off we go!

—Lynn Arave and Ray Boren

— PART I. —

MYSTERIOUS PLACES

1

NAVAJO MOUNTAIN

Sacred—and Remote

I n isolated southeastern Utah—where red rock, a wrinkled landscape and open air rule—and located somewhere between Forbidding Canyon and No Man Mesa is perhaps the state's most mysterious mountain. Many who see it rising on the horizon likely don't even know its name; others are unaware that this geologic prominence is even in Utah, for it is close to the Arizona border.

A mammoth mound, Navajo Mountain is a high-elevation (peaking at 10,388 feet above sea level), rounded dome. From a distance it resembles a whale's back, rising in this case above a sea of sandstone. It is the area's dominant landmark, almost 7,000 feet above and east of Lake Powell on the Navajo Indian Reservation. Want a strong cell phone signal on southern Lake Powell? You will likely have that only if Navajo Mountain is in sight, since cell towers crown its top.

The peak is also perhaps the most sacred mountain in southern Utah. It is blessed with above-it-all solitude and solace. To even get to Navajo Mountain requires more than one hundred miles of driving through extreme northern Arizona first and then heading north into the Beehive State.

Leo Manheimer, a chapter president of the Navajo Mountain Chapter House that sits on the southeast side of the mountain, has said it is one of four sacred mountains in the region. "It's the highest point in the Navajo Nation boundaries," he said.

Sacred to religious Navajos—including some who believe it shouldn't be summited—the mountain, in Utah's San Juan County, is fewer than three

Ravell Call (*far left*) and Ray Boren on Navajo Mountain, far above the Colorado River's Lake Powell and southern Utah's wrinkled landscape. *Lynn Arave photo.*

miles from Rainbow Bridge, another sacred Indian site. For more than a fifty-mile radius, Navajo Mountain is the preeminent natural feature.

According to *Navajo Places: History, Legend and Landscape*, by Laurance D. Linford, in certain Navajo beliefs the mountain is head of the sacred Earth Mother, and it is key to the sacred pollen range for the Navajo people, the Dené. Indeed, tradition-minded Navajos believe that other geological features scattered over the region represent some of her other body parts. Black Mesa is her body, the Balakai Mesa her feet, Comb Ridge an arm. Agathia Peak and Tuba Butte are her breasts. Navajo Mountain figures into other tales, as well. "Place of Rising" and "Flint Hogan" are individual sacred places atop its summits.

As a laccolithic dome—an irregular, uplifted formation of igneous rock—Navajo Mountain is of volcanic origin, though a layman might never think so simply by looking at it. Some of the only volcanic rock visible is on the mountaintop's north end. Shattered sandstone surrounds it.

Linford reported that traditional Navajos are reluctant to climb the peak and some fear underground rumblings on its west slope. It wasn't until the 1940s that most Navajos would go north of the mountain into what is now the canyon country of Lake Powell National Recreation Area and Canyonlands National Park.

Neighboring Paiute Indians, on the other hand, would travel the region with no hesitation. In fact, before 1933, the mountain was generally known as "Paiute Mountain."

Navajo Mountain is ignored by most peak-climbing "high pointers" and hikers, since you can travel a rugged nine-mile, four-wheel-drive road to its forested summit and because it sits inside the Navajo Reservation.

Despite its isolation and prominence, the humpy mountain might not be deemed as spectacular as others of its ilk, for it lacks jagged summits. Nor is it a county high point, and hence a peak to "bag" on standard lists of outdoor accomplishments. Navajo is, as a rule, not featured in Utah or regional hiking guides or books.

Much more popular today is the Rainbow Bridge trail, which skirts the north side of Navajo Mountain and provides access to this famed natural formation near, and usually via, Lake Powell. (And, yes, Rainbow Bridge is readily visible with the naked eye when peering down from the summit's north end—if you look carefully enough.)

But a trip up Navajo Mountain ultimately isn't about conquest or peak bagging. It might be more about stirring views of the magnificent territory around it and perhaps feeling a connection with mountain and land, as Navajos might attest.

You don't get where you want to go in this territory without knowing exactly where you're going. The region is famed for its maze of sandstone river channels and slot canyons, and the entire area is saturated in legend, including rumors of an old Native American silver mine said to be situated somewhere just south of Navajo Mountain.

Snow graces the upper elevations in winter and even into spring. A trip up Navajo should never be attempted in wet or threatening weather, as the road becomes impassible when wet.

Accessing the mountain requires a roundabout route northward from Arizona, between Monument Valley and Page. Between the small Navajo communities of Kaibito and Shonto, just off Arizona Highway 98, you turn north into Utah. Even then, visitors are not allowed to traverse the remote area at will. A backcountry permit (with a fee) is required by the Navajo Nation to leave the main roads.

However, "Welcom [*sic*] white man" is painted on a rock on the way up Navajo Mountain.

The upper portion of the rugged and rocky back-road trail leading to the top of Navajo Mountain. *Lynn Arave photo.*

The rough road to and up the peak passes near War God Springs, on a nine-thousand-foot-elevation plateau. The steep track includes high switchbacks that sometimes are so sharp that motorists have to back up and do two passes to negotiate the hairpin turns. The path is littered with loose stones, some of which might be better described as mini boulders.

Finally, a hike of about three-fourths of a mile, to the north, is necessary along the summit ridge to get past a set of transmission towers and maintenance trailers to a viewpoint where the trees clear and reveal Rainbow Bridge and Lake Powell, visible far below amid a corrugated landscape.

Rainbow Bridge only exists thanks to Navajo Mountain. Over many eons, water runoff in a drainage from Navajo Mountain carved the massive natural bridge.

Mountains to the south, like Navajo, are forested at higher elevations, with a higher tree line than their northern counterparts. Indeed, there is forest here at the top, more than ten thousand feet up. At the summit, the pristine atmosphere is incredibly serene and peaceful, the commanding views rivaled only by those available from an airplane.

While high-profile off-road vehicles might have the clearance to negotiate and miss most of the loose rocks on the road going up the mountain, coming back down is a different story. Because portions of the road are so steep—probably a 16 percent grade—braking will lower that clearance slightly. Someone might have to get out of the vehicle and toss rocks off the narrow, jeep "trail" on the way down.

Navajo Mountain is also the name of the tiny, isolated reservation community located on the southeast side of the peak. Occasionally, jokes are made about Park City and Moab not really being "Utah towns," based on their social and religious differences when compared with most other municipalities in the Beehive State. In contrast, Navajo Mountain's trading post, schools, Navajo Nation tribal office and U.S. post office are all at least three to five miles *within* Utah—but that's all there is of Utah about it.

The vast majority of vehicles you will spot in Navajo Mountain sport Arizona license plates.

The area code, 928, is Arizona based.

The post office lists the locality as being in Arizona instead of Utah. Page, Arizona, is the nearest town of a significant size.

The little town of Navajo Mountain, tucked away below its namesake sacred peak, doesn't even pretend it is in Utah.

2

RAINBOW BRIDGE

"Lore" and "Found"

Rainbow Bridge, a magnificent water-carved natural arch sacred to the Navajos, is so remote that it wasn't "discovered" until 1909, by a party led by a university professor and government surveyor—and they depended on the help of Indian guides to find it.

Rainbow is one of the largest known natural bridges in the world, arching some 275 feet across and 246 feet above the entrenched canyon below, according to the National Park Service. Many references point out that the U.S. Capitol would fit beneath the span.

Undoubtedly known by prehistoric people and neighboring American Indian tribal members, the bridge might have first been seen by people of European descent in the 1880s, during a gold rush in the Colorado River's Glen Canyon. Miners swarmed the area seeking the precious metal and likely ventured up its canyon. Cowboys might have encountered the bridge. None of them, however, seemed compelled to share the news of this startling geologic oddity with the rest of the country.

Rainbow Bridge brochures and Park Service studies note that it was more permanently "discovered" on August 14, 1909. Byron Cummings, dean of arts and sciences at the University of Utah, and William B. Douglass, a government surveyor, had heard rumors of a great stone arch and set out from Kayenta, Arizona, at the same time, leading separate exploration parties. Eventually, they combined forces and were led to the landmark by Jim Mike (then known as Mike's Boy), a Paiute, and Nasja-Begay, variously described as a Paiute and a Navajo. Jim Mike—who lived over a century,

Rainbow Bridge is an isolated natural wonder between Lake Powell and Navajo Mountain. *Ray Boren photo.*

passing away in 1977—is now generally credited with finding the massive bridge in about 1900, while seeking pasture for a herd of horses.

Publicity following the Cummings-Douglass expedition gave Rainbow Bridge, tucked away in an obscure canyon below Navajo Mountain in the midst of the desolate Colorado Plateau, international renown. With remarkable speed by modern standards, President William Howard Taft proclaimed the wonder a national monument, setting aside a 160-acre tract on May 30, 1910.

Writer Zane Grey and former president and sometime-adventurer Theodore Roosevelt visited the remote span separately during horseback and camping expeditions in 1913. Other excursions, often led by Four Corners guide John Wetherill, followed over the years, in and out of little canyons and over desert sandstone humps.

Modern visitors, though, usually approach Rainbow Bridge aboard an excursion boat out of Lake Powell National Recreation Area's southern marinas. Neither the lake nor the marinas, of course, existed in the early twentieth century.

Roland Muenzen captained one such a craft, the *Desert Reflection*, as it delicately threaded its way through Forbidding Canyon toward Bridge

Canyon. "All of these canyons have one thing in common," he told his passengers, "one way in and one way out."

One of the Rainbow Bridge's earliest adventurous tourists was Charles L. Bernheimer, a self-described "tenderfoot and cliff dweller from Manhattan," who wrote about his amateur explorations of "Rainbow Bridge country" in a 1926 book named for the span. As with the Grand Canyon or Niagara Falls, he considered it futile to compare this scenic landmark with any other marvel. He did, however, offer a description:

> *The dimensions of the Rainbow Bridge, its symmetry, its graceful sweep, its delicate balance, its daintiness, despite its bulk, its picturesque setting and colouring, make it an unique and stupendous monument. It is beautiful from whatever angle it is seen. How has this gem in high relief, carved as by a divine hand, withstood destruction by the very forces which reared it? Imagine a structure the evolutions of the ages have merely brought to the surface its muscular structure, divesting it of weak and useless particles. Where the strain is greatest, its contour suggests the arm and shoulders of a trained athlete. Where the weight rests on abutments, the latter suggest the virile forms of fluted, supporting Gothic pillars.*

The region's Indians, including the San Juan Paiutes and White Mesa Paiutes, but especially the Navajos, consider Rainbow Bridge to be sacred. "They want people to understand that this is to them a place of worship and want people to treat it as they would their own places of worship," an interpretive park ranger explained during one journey to the natural bridge.

To the Navajos, the ranger said, Navajo Mountain nearby is the head of the Earth Mother; the sun is the father. Two other holy figures also play key roles. "Monster Slayer and Child Born of the Water, children of Changing Woman, never met their father, the sun. They held a ceremony, building a rainbow of many materials between the Material World and the Spirit World."

The legend's description fits Rainbow Bridge.

Before the 1909 discovery, Douglass had tried and failed to reach the natural bridge earlier in 1908. Initially in the early 1900s, a Native American could not be found who had actually seen the bridge. It required an extensive search all one winter to find a knowledgeable guide, according to the *Salt Lake Herald* newspaper of June 3, 1910.

The *Salt Lake Herald-Republican* of September 5, 1909, was one of many newspapers that recorded Douglass's description on first successfully reaching and seeing the bridge:

Tourists can crowd around Rainbow Bridge at times, even though the arch is sacred to many Native Americans. *Ray Boren photo.*

At a quarter past 11 o'clock a shout from those in front told the rest that the bridge was in sight. The drooping spirits freshened and the last few hundred yards were made with lighter hearts. The first view was wonderful. The great stone arch lay deep in the shadow of overhanging cliffs. Red on its face and purple in its shadows, it presented a striking picture—a pleasant contrast to the hot, sunbaked sands of the preceding three days. As the party drew near it, its magnitude dawned upon its members. Its greatness was awful. The party stood in open-mouthed amazement. The first impression of these great works of nature can never be forgotten.

A wagon road was not completed into the Navajo Mountain area until 1925, so discovering the bridge was a true adventure in 1908–10. Even today the area is isolated. Rainbow Bridge is twelve miles northwest of Navajo Mountain, the ten-thousand-plus-foot-high peak that dominates the landscape.

"Hole in the Rock Shaped Liked a Rainbow" was a Navajo name for the sacred arch. From it, tradition says, come rainbows, clouds and moisture for the reservation. Today visitors are asked to be sensitive to Native

American beliefs and to not walk under the arch, let alone climb it, as has happened in the past.

Rainbow Bridge was a focus of debate over the proposed construction by the U.S. Bureau of Reclamation of a dam on the Colorado River to create Lake Powell in the 1950s. It was argued that the backup of water as the new lake filled would flood Bridge Canyon and damage the arch. Special backwater dams were initially proposed to protect the arch and national monument, but ultimately, it was determined they might damage the feature more than the impounded river water would.

So, Glen Canyon Dam was built as planned, a great plug on the Colorado River, and after June 1963, the rising lake began to approach Rainbow Bridge. This made the once truly remote natural bridge accessible by boat as a day trip, usually with a short hike from a moveable dock to reach the wonder—all in far contrast to the wanderings and explorations of Native Americans, prospectors, cowboys, professorial explorers and adventurers of an earlier day.

NOAH'S ARK

In Southern Utah?

The search for Noah's Ark has sparked many an ambitious expedition or documentary over the years. However, some forty miles from Zion National Park is Utah's own Noah's Ark—its official name on government maps.

This isn't the real ark, of course, but an intriguing cliff-top, ship-shaped formation, distinguished by its red, or vermillion, coloration. It is located about five miles southeast of Parowan on the south side of First Left Hand Canyon, at an elevation of 8,592 feet above sea level.

Approaching 1,000 feet in length, this Noah's Ark is about twice the estimated length of the biblical boat, which is commonly said to be at least 300 cubits (a cubit is believed to be 18 inches long) or about 550 feet long and 45 feet high.

Utah's Noah's Ark hasn't received much attention in newspapers and other publications over the decades. An early mention was in the *Parowan Times* newspaper of December 2, 1938. That story discussed a new forest camp and ranger station being built in the area, near the "Ark" formation.

Who named the boat-like rock for Noah's craft, and when, is lost to time. Dixie National Forest, in which it is found, has no additional information specifically about the Noah's Ark Trail.

Bruce Matheson, a Parowan resident, said the formation is a landmark for all locals in the canyons. He doesn't know where the name came from. Its origin is not mentioned in the history books, and it is just assumed that some early settler started calling it Noah's Ark, and the name stuck.

Utah's Noah's Ark is a high rock formation that early settlers believed resembled the biblical ark. *Lynn Arave photo.*

A marked trail begins in the Vermillion picnic area and leads to a closer view of Noah's Ark. However, the view from the road and picnic area is OK.

Although signs say the trail is 1.0 mile long, one way, it is closer to 1.5 miles long. The path climbs steeply in places, starting from an elevation of 6,927 feet above sea level and topping out at 8,037 feet—for a total climb of 1,110 feet. There is some shade along the trail, but it is not one to do in the heat of a summer day. The trail ends on a small plateau that also offers a view of the Little Salt Lake and the surrounding area.

Nearby is Grand Castle, a kingly red-rock formation to the north of Noah's Ark. To the west and near the canyon floor is Vermillion Castle.

"The Parowan area has some of the most gorgeous rock formations around," Matheson said. "The colors are very vivid." He's heard of a few hikers and climbers over the years who have managed to get to the top of Noah's Ark, though it looks to be a steep and risky climb.

Mike Ward, who lives in Paragonah, describes Noah's Ark and its surroundings as spectacular. "The whole area is a stunner," he said. Second Left Hand Canyon, to the south, is his favorite destination—especially since

The trailhead to Noah's Ark, in southwest Utah, is in Dixie National Forest near Parowan, Utah. *Lynn Arave photo.*

it has a mountain bike trail that connects with Brian Head, a mountain, resort and community high above, near Cedar Breaks National Monument.

The Parowan Canyon area is home to a slew of other oddly shaped—and named—features. There's room to contemplate in Free Thought Canyon, as well as Squaw Hollow, Hole in the Rock, Billy West Canyon and Yankee Meadows.

And for romantics there is Valentine Peak. When the sun rises each February 14, it perfectly aligns with the summit, as seen from downtown Parowan. If you're in the right place and frame of mind.

NINE MILE CANYON

Art Gallery in Stone

I n the not so distant past, someone came up with an apt description of Utah's Nine Mile Canyon, proclaiming it the "world's longest art gallery."

What Nine Mile really is, of course, is a beautifully rugged desert oasis, generously decorated with petroglyphs and pictographs—one thousand or more "rock art" panels composed of even more thousands of individual images. These were pecked and painted onto the canyon's tan sandstone walls from one thousand or more years ago to more recent times by Native Americans, primarily a pre-Columbian people we call the Fremont but also by more modern Utes. Scores of sites in the canyon and its tributaries are listed on the National Register of Historic Places.

The culture's name comes from central Utah's Fremont River, along which some of the people lived, and thus from the nineteenth-century American explorer John Charles Frémont. We don't know what the Fremont called themselves during their ancient heyday, about AD 900–1300. That four-hundred-year span coincided with the Ancestral Pueblo, or Anasazi, of the Colorado River/Four Corners region, where the borders of Arizona, New Mexico, Colorado and Utah meet.

Like the Southwest's prehistoric Pueblo peoples, the Fremont hunted and foraged, grew corn and squash and made and used stone and wooden tools, pottery, baskets and wonderful artifacts, such as the Pilling figurines, small human figures molded from unbaked clay, found in the nearby Range Creek area. Other evidence of the Fremont culture includes scattered ruins, such as pit-houses and granaries built high on cliffs.

Nine Mile Canyon in central Utah is actually more like fifty miles long. Its name origin is a mystery. *Ray Boren photo.*

We also are not really certain why it is called Nine Mile Canyon, for the corridor is really almost fifty miles long, with a set of side canyons that are also prime palettes for pictographic art. Our friend archaeologist Jerry D. Spangler has researched that question and mentions it in several books about the canyon and region, including *Horned Snakes and Axle Grease*, a guide about Nine Mile Canyon written with his wife, Donna K. Spangler; *Last Chance Byway*; and *Crimson Cowboys*, about an early archaeology expedition, written with James M. Aton. Spangler says the name probably comes from a mapping mistake.

The John Wesley Powell journals of 1869 and 1871, when he led parties down the Green and Colorado Rivers, mention a creek by that name but "are actually referring to Rock Creek in the heart of Desolation Canyon, which happens to be about nine miles long," Spangler says. Another possibility is a stretch that freighters called Nine Mile Valley along the canyon's rough road, a route overall that bedeviled them, their wagons and animals in the late 1800s. "I found a couple of early map references to that," Spangler says. "It is not outlandish that the freighters simply applied the name to the entire creek" and thus the canyon.

Checking out the rock art and ruins of Nine Mile can be a delightful exploration for a day or a lifetime. It is one of Utah's best and most accessible such "galleries," which also include places like Fremont Indian State Park on I-70; Parowan Gap; Newspaper Rock, near Canyonlands National Park's Needles District; Canyonland's impressive but remote Great Gallery in Horseshoe Canyon; the Rochester Panel, near Emery, Utah; the private McConkie Ranch, near Vernal; and many more.

For major sites in Nine Mile Canyon, promoters at some point put up markers, with signs placed high on poles, arrows pointing to a prehistoric artwork or artifact, such as "First Site," a "Granary" and the "Daddy Canyon Complex." The Bureau of Land Management, the State of Utah, county governments, volunteer coalitions and even resource-extracting corporations have helped put in place informational signs, as well as scattered picnic areas and restrooms.

Accessed most directly from the south, out of Wellington, along US 6 but also from the north, going south, outside of Myton along US 40, visiting Nine Mile is like physically entering an illustrated bestiary—a book of beasts—because of its many rock-art animals and birds. That seems appropriate, because the "bestiary vocabulum" is a richly illustrated volume featuring creatures—some real, others fantasies—especially popular during medieval times. Coincidentally, that is about the same time frame as the Fremont.

There are thousands of petroglyphs and pictographs in the Nine Mile Canyon area, including the Great Hunt Panel. *Ray Boren photo.*

During drives and exploratory hikes, we've come across wonderful panels, sometimes of marvelous intricacy. Visitors encounter depictions of angular, big-shouldered humans (often called anthropomorphs), some with impressive headwear and weapons; great numbers of big-horn sheep; human hands and bear claws; bison, deer and elk; owls and sandhill cranes—and a fair number of long, zig-zaggy snakes, often with horns on their heads.

Occasionally, you'll espy the figure of a horse, maybe with a rider. This would obviously be a sight witnessed and recorded on rock by Utes, not earlier Fremont people, after the arrival in previously horseless western North America of Spanish conquistadors and explorers in the 1500s— the Dominguez-Escalante expedition out of Santa Fe passed nearby in 1776—and especially fur trappers, traders and settlers of European descent in the 1800s.

The best known of the Nine Mile complex's petroglyph panels is The Great Hunt. The National Park Service describes the site, around a bend in offshoot Cottonwood Canyon, as a "prehistoric artistic expression," displaying "religious behavior and hunting behavior." The artfully composed panel, pecked into the patina of a buff-to-red wall, features an eye-catching array—a herd?—of about thirty bighorn sheep and eight human-like figures, several with bows and arrows. It has been interpreted as a communal hunt.

Elsewhere, in a shallow alcove, is another notable pictograph, depicting what appears to be a rotund elk with long, spiky antlers, created with red pigment. Unfortunately, in decades past, someone painted or stenciled, in blocky black capital letters, right atop the creature:

THIS IS PRIVATE PROPERTY
NO TRESSPASSING

(Yes, they added an extra *s* to *trespassing*.)

Honoring property rights in the canyon is, nevertheless, the proper thing to do.

The mysterious Fremont era is not the only human history of Nine Mile Canyon. By the late 1800s, it was an important freight and stagecoach route from central Utah trails and later railheads through the Tavaputs Plateau north to Fort Duchesne and the Uintah Basin. It served as headquarters for major cattle ranching operations in the late nineteenth and early twentieth centuries, a tradition that somewhat continues to this day. It is now key to oil and natural gas exploration and pumping on the plateau, which brings big trucks to Nine Mile's serpentine and recently paved road.

Besides petroglyphs and ancient ruins, Nine Mile Canyon is sprinkled in places with old homesteads, left-behind antique trucks and cars, old military outbuildings and modern farm equipment. Cowboys, prospectors and other passersby also scratched or scrawled their names with grease on canyon walls.

Ultimately, there is also the natural beauty of Nine Mile Canyon itself: time-streaked sandstone cliffs and pinnacles, offset in the creek's bottomlands by majestic cottonwood trees and green pastures or fields of alfalfa and grass. And balanced precariously right above the road on a high rock shelf is a boulder that looks remarkably like the head of Porky Pig.

You never know what you'll come across while exploring Utah's ancient oasis Nine Mile Canyon.

5

THE PANDO CLONE

Many from One

I n 2006, the U.S. Postal Service published a colorful sheet of postage stamps (thirty-nine cents in those days) celebrating forty different Wonders of America, subtitled Land of Superlatives. In a philatelic parade that included the "oldest" and the "tallest" and the "deepest" in various natural and manmade ways, one stamp spotlighted the white trunks of a quaking aspen grove. Lettering on it said, "Largest plant."

Though the illustrated stamp didn't include the grove's name per se, it was honoring Pando, a grove just southwest of central Utah's high Fish Lake (elevation 8,848 feet). The name is a Latin word meaning "I spread," as Americans and Utahns—most of whom had never previously heard of Pando—and stamp aficionados around the world would learn.

Scientists had selected the name because Pando began life as a single seed and expanded over 106 acres to include forty to fifty thousand trees, which sprouted from a vast root system that sends up shoots or suckers—natural cloning. That first seed is believed to have germinated sometime during last Pleistocene Ice Age, perhaps about eighty thousand years ago by one estimate, making Pando both one of the largest and oldest living things on Earth, at least as far as researchers can say. There might be even bigger aspen clones out there not yet discovered and genetically tested like Pando, and other organisms might indeed be older, scientists hedge.

But one of the amazing things about Pando that is you can drive right up to and through it on Utah Highway 25, accessed between the small towns of Koosharem and Loa off the more-traveled Utah Highway 24.

A mix of aspen trees during the fall season in the Pando Aspen Grove near Fish Lake. *Ray Boren photo.*

Recent signs tell motorists that they are "entering the Pando Aspen Clone." And while some of the aspen trees are fenced off, especially west of the highway, in an effort to study and preserve this remarkable grove, you can walk and hike and even camp here, under the stars and the shivering leaves. And as the name of the large lake implies, there is a lot of fishing going on in the vicinity.

As a nearby interpretive history display points out, the grove is also astride the "Old Spanish Trail," a 1,200-mile nineteenth-century route linking Santa Fe, now the capital of New Mexico, and Alta California's Pueblo de Los Angeles, better known as L.A.

A string of black cut-metal silhouettes depicts men riding horses, leading pack-laden mules. "Between 1829 and 1848," a placard explains, "traders used the trail to carry New Mexican woolen goods—rugs, blankets and serapes—that were traded for California mules and horses." The trail made a big curve northward to avoid the impassable Grand Canyon and other chasms of the Colorado Plateau to the south.

Like similar swaths of aspen in Fish Lake National Forest, Pando is particularly beautiful in autumn, when leaves of the quaking aspen (*Populus tremuloides*) tremble in even a light breeze and shimmer in the sunlight of a clear blue sky.

However, despite its size and moderate fame, many are concerned about Pando's present and future. Forest personnel and researchers first understood the grove's unusual size and age in the 1970s and soon realized that the aged aspen stand is in poor health.

"It's not necessarily that the overstory is dying, or some of the clone is not doing well, but we're not getting any regeneration to replace those parts that are dying," silviculturist Terrance Holsclaw says in a Fishlake National Forest video about the Pando clone, posted on YouTube.

Dying trees are not unusual among aspen, but groves are usually able to continue to grow and replace those trees. Good old Pando hasn't been doing well at this, and other factors are also playing a part in the decline, the Forest Service says. Researchers have found that insects, such as bark beetles and other borers, and diseases are killing trees. Browsing mule deer and other grazing animals have also had free rein, likely nibbling most new sprouts before they can grow enough to become replacement trees.

In 2019, the Western Watersheds Project, a group advocating less livestock grazing on public lands, more specifically pointed the blame here on range cattle. In autumn, about one thousand domestic cows and calves pass through Pando and the forest at large, moving from high summer pastures to lower ones for winter. Using motion-detecting cameras in Pando and other groves, the project posits that about 90 percent of the unfenced plants under the aspens are consumed by the cattle, the *Salt Lake Tribune* reported.

To help Pando, fencing now keeps the grazing herbivores away from a large portion of the grove to see if that helps foster new growth, the Forest Service says. Researchers are also studying roles played by root rot, heart rot and other diseases, molds and fungus problems, as well as bacteria.

Aspen groves also do better in disturbed soil, so controlled burns have been prescribed in places, and competing junipers and other types of undergrowth are being removed by the Forest Service and its partners. With such treatments and methods, the forest's managers and researchers have been attempting to stem or reverse Pando's decline and encourage new sprouting.

The foresters are trying to learn from the ancient aspen grove itself—and to help it adapt to the invading world.

6

CHINATOWN

Red Rock in Northern Utah

There are "strange rock formations and colors of much scenic value" in northern Utah's Chinatown, an article reported in the *Ogden Standard-Examiner* on October 13, 1931. The story was headlined "Scenic Route Fund Desired." O.A. Taylor of Brigham City, it seems, had interest in a coal mine in that out-of-the-way area—but he also believed this "Chinatown" might prove a desirable tourist attraction.

His proposals and plans, though, never materialized. And to the present day, this almost forgotten red-rock Chinatown remains inaccessible, tucked away on private land, closed to sightseeing and picture-taking and postcard-buying.

Strictly speaking, and according to most dictionaries, a "Chinatown" is an enclave or neighborhood in a generally non-Asian urban community that is dominated by residents of Chinese or sometimes other Asian origin and ethnicity. Northern Utah's Chinatown, however, is a work of nature in mostly rural and agricultural Morgan County and about ten miles northeast of Henefer, Summit County, which sits beside Interstate 84 along the Weber River.

This little-known Chinatown received its name because its natural formations—eroded from conglomerate rock—reminded pioneer visitors of Asian pagodas, towering and ornate structures that are several stories high. Other hoodoo-like formations are shaped more like Indian totem poles.

Several miles north of Chinatown are separate sections of unusual rock that are more reminiscent of Idaho's granite City of Rocks and even

Chinatown, a remote natural wonder on private land, is seemingly a slice of southern Utah red rock in northern Utah. *Lynn Arave photo.*

southwestern Utah's national parks. Similar carved conglomerate features, like the Temple Rock Amphitheater, are visible along I-84 and its frontage road near the little junction town of Echo—and Echo Canyon, hosting Interstate 80 between Echo and Evanston, Wyoming, is itself lined with awesome red cliffs.

Chinatown's allure and potential resulted in repeated journalistic comment over the years.

A *Standard-Examiner* story from February 2, 1932, noted that both the Morgan and the Ogden Lions clubs supported a scenic highway to Chinatown through Toone Canyon, off Lost Creek Road. Ogden mayor Ora Bundy said in that story that Chinatown rivaled the scenery of red-rock southern Utah. He also favored a loop road so that Ogden Valley could be reached from the Morgan County side.

Chinatown sits atop the northern walls of Weber Canyon, not visible from Interstate 84 below. *Lynn Arave photo.*

The Richfield Reaper newspaper of June 19, 1930, called Chinatown "a fascinating curiosity shop of mother nature." It stated that some of the rock formations had been given evocative names: Japanese Teapot, Alligator Rock, 11 Apostles, Sea Rock, Yellow Dike, Twin Elephants, Big Elephant and Newfoundland Dog. In nearby Toone Canyon are Red Ridge and Totem Pole.

A June 14, 1936 article in the *Salt Lake Tribune* proclaimed Chinatown to be a "geological wonder." It said an early nickname for the area had been "Hidden Towers." In another report a few years later, the *Standard* reported on January 30, 1938, that about "12 miles northeast of Devil's Slide is a natural curiosity known as 'Chinatown.' It is a miniature Bryce Canyon with many shades of rock."

Then Chinatown faded into obscurity for almost three decades, until an editorial in the November 19, 1965 *Standard* heralded its attractions once again. "The eroded cliffs of Morgan's 'Chinatown' closely resemble the famed earthen spires and pinnacles of Bryce Canyon National Park," the editorial declared. It urged a three-man committee in Morgan to find a way to open it to the public.

According to Fred Ulrich, the Morgan High School Latter-day Saints Seminary sponsored an annual spring hike to Chinatown, at least into the late 1940s.

The tiny town of Croydon, between Henefer and Morgan, highlighted Chinatown's scenic value and suggested allowing visitors as recently as the early 1960s.

Although Chinatown presently remains off-limits to the general public, co-author Lynn Arave was fortunate to secure permission to check out Chinatown in 1990. The rare visit required some eight miles of mountain bicycling and about six hiking miles, resulting in a 2,000-foot-plus climb to access the formation, located near the Morgan-Summit county line and overlooking Interstate 84. The trek involved passing through four locked gates and multiple tracts of private land to reach the thirteen-acre site, at an elevation of 7,800 feet above sea level.

Comparisons to the red-rock parks of southern Utah are clear. Chinatown is more like a miniature Cedar Breaks National Monument, perhaps, than a section of Bryce Canyon National Park. It certainly seems out of place in mountainous northern Utah and more typical of the incised plateaus of southern Utah. Eroded red pinnacles—two to three hundred feet tall—rise amid a scenic background of quaking aspen and evergreens.

The idea, as suggested almost a century ago, that Chinatown might be worthy of being set aside for its scenic value, perhaps as a state park, certainly springs to mind. But that concept isn't likely to be favored by the area's landowners.

Indeed, much of Chinatown's current attraction is its isolation and solitude—assets that would surely vanish with public access.

7

PETER SINKS

Hyper-Cold Dip

H ow cold is sixty-nine degrees below zero?

A little and remote mountain valley, located about five miles northwest of the Bear Lake Summit along US 89, is deemed the coldest spot in Utah—and one of the most frigid in the lower forty-eight states.

In Peter Sinks, the thermometer dipped to negative 69.3 degrees on February 1, 1985—the all-time record for the coldest known temperature in the Beehive State. Only Rogers Pass in Montana apparently has measured a lower reading in the contiguous forty-eight states, dropping to negative 69.7 degrees in January 1954.

Many lists of the nation's cold places only highlight towns and not isolated places like Peter Sinks—and other rankings only consider measurements recorded at official National Weather Service stations. By those standards, Peter Sinks's big drop is "unofficial." No one lives there, and the reading was not from a certified National Weather Service station at the time.

Nevertheless, Peter Sinks continues to be one of the nation's best-known natural iceboxes. For instance, on the morning of October 30, 2019, Peter Sinks recorded the lowest October temperature ever recorded by the National Weather Service for any of the lower forty-eight states, at minus 45.5 degrees. This occurred during a record-breaking cold spell in the western and midwestern states, when frigid Arctic air spilled down south as far as Arizona.

Just what is a "sink," and why does it get so cold here, high above Bear Lake, which is divided by the Utah-Idaho state line?

Scott Steele examines the automated National Weather Service Station at the bottom of Peter Sinks. *Lynn Arave photo.*

Peter Sinks is an alpine sinkhole, sitting at an elevation of 8,092 feet above sea level. It is large, about a mile long and three-fourths of a mile wide. Nearby Logan Canyon and the Bear River Mountains here are mostly limestone and are riddled with underground caverns and caves. Limestone, a sedimentary rock formed from marine organisms such as shellfish and coral, is therefore mostly composed of calcium carbonate and calcite. These can dissolve over time, due to acids and water. When resulting cavities in the rock collapse, the surface may subside, and sinks, or sinkholes, dips and depressions, are born.

There are more than three dozen known caves in a fifteen-mile radius around Peter Sinks, including closed and gated Logan Cave and, farther away, Minnetonka Cave, above St. Charles, Idaho, where guided tours are conducted in the summertime.

Peter Sinks is similar to the more accessible Middle and Upper Sinks, visible to the south alongside US 89 as it climbs to the Bear Lake overlook summit. They are extra cold places, too, but not quite as cold as Peter Sinks. In fact, *sink* and *sinks* are common appellations throughout this area of upper Logan Canyon. There's a North Sink and a South Sink, as well as a Sinker, all found on pertinent U.S. Geological Survey (USGS) maps.

The sinks and dimples help make the area a snowmobile haven in wintertime and part of an ATV loop ride in summer. Deer hunters and ranchers occasionally visit more remote Peter Sinks, and cattle seasonally roam the range.

As do those fascinated by the weather.

Peter Sinks and its legendary cold were discovered in the early 1980s by Zane Stephens, who worked in Logan for Utah State University Climatology at the time, and a friend, Mike Bowman. They were specifically seeking the coldest spot in Utah.

First, they checked out Dry Lake in Sardine Canyon, along US 89 southwest of Logan. It was cold there but not usually subzero. Then they found some European research on sinks and began to search those. They found Middle and Upper Sinks in Logan Canyon to be below zero at times and realized that if a higher elevation sink was in that area, it could be the kingpin of them all.

Peter Sinks is located over two low summits to the south of Middle Sinks. Stephens and Bowman found that the spot fit their criteria, and they made Utah weather history when they recorded that frigid negative sixty-nine degree reading in 1985. Local Utah TV meteorologists helped popularize chilly Peter Sinks's notoriety in succeeding years and now decades.

Why is it so frigid in these Utah sinks?

Cold can simply be defined as the absence of heat. And cold air will always settle in the lowest place. All it takes for record-cold temperatures in these sinks and sinkholes is a temperature inversion, a good and icy snowpack, a lack of wind and a long winter night.

A lone, dwarf pine tree (*left*) greets visitors as they descend into the bottom of Peter Sinks. No trees can live at the bottom. *Lynn Arave photo.*

A sink will act somewhat like a reservoir for subsiding cold air, scientists say. The temperature at the bottom of Peter Sinks might be as many as fifteen to twenty degrees colder than the air at the top of its rim. That is because cold air is so dense that it pools and can be trapped easily in these sinks. This extra-cold air is also why no trees and little vegetation can survive inside these sinkholes. That is also how the chilly characteristics of these sinks were discovered—weather researchers actually felt the cold air as it leaked out from such depressions.

Thermometers have been known to freeze solid inside Peter Sinks while trying to capture alarmingly low readings of its frigid air, as researchers learned in the early 1980s, shortly after it was discovered. And since these sinkholes are still sinking, they might become somewhat colder in the future.

Even in summer, Peter Sinks can be a pretty cool place. For example, one summer day some years ago, it was ninety-nine degrees in Logan but only eighty-four in Peter Sinks. On August 27, 2020, Logan was in the low nineties for a high, while Peter Sinks was about sixty-eight degrees.

No one lives anywhere near Peter Sinks, and with good reason—probably not even "Peter," whoever he was. The location was already named on USGS maps for the mysterious Peter decades before 1985, when Peter Sinks gained frosty fame.

Was there a Peter who frequented the area? Cattle roam this area in summer. Was Peter an early rancher or cowboy, perhaps in the nineteenth century? The usually helpful book *Utah Place Names*, by John W. Van Cott, lists Peter Sinks but supplies no information or even theories about the appellation's origin. Is there a notable person named Peter in Cache County or Rich County history? No one has readily and reliably found one that seems applicable.

Except, according to an Associated Press story by Judy Fahys, published in the *Daily Spectrum* on April 30, 2010, Peter Sinks might be named after a miner who once tried to homestead the place and froze to death. "When he didn't show up after a nasty winter, goes the third-hand account, a search party from Bear Lake went looking for him. The party found him frozen to death."

The fact that there is a "Deadman Gulch" listed on USGS maps less than two miles northeast of Peter Sinks might add support to a settler named Peter freezing to death in the area during the 1800s. There's no verified history for that geographic feature either, but it is close to Peter Sinks.

Here's an even wilder possible tie into the name: Biblically, it is a stretch, but the apostle Peter "sank" in the waters of the Sea of Galilee while trying to walk on water (Matthew 14), until Jesus lifted him up. There is no lake in Peter Sinks, but cold air sinks there at times. And to the west of Peter Sinks, straight north of Logan Canyon and about eight air miles distant are the biblically named Gog and Magog peaks—and not far away from there is Mount Naomi, another biblical name and the highest point in Cache County. And another biblically derived name, Sadducee Spring, is also nearby, in upper Logan Canyon.

The possibilities seem endless.

PART II

LEGENDS OF UTAH'S PAST

8

A REAL HOWARD STARK

He Died in Utah

Mention Howard Stark to anyone today and they might instantly think of the fictional Howard Stark from the Marvel comics and movie universe, who was the late father of Iron Man, alias of Tony Stark. But a real Howard Stark actually existed, who was both a legendary pilot and an inventor—and he died in the aftermath of a plane crash in northern Utah.

A headline in the *Salt Lake Tribune* from June 16, 1936, read, "Search party follows lost U.S. flier's trail for five miles. Major Stark wandered down Lost Creek from plane after crack-up last January." So, there was a real Howard Stark who piloted airplanes in the early decades of the twenteith century!

Stark flew U.S. mail in airplanes. He was flying from Rock Springs, Wyoming, to Salt Lake City on January 16, 1936, when all radio contact was lost. A winter storm apparently forced him to crash-land on a remote Utah mountain, Observatory Peak, twenty-eight miles northeast of Devil's Slide and east of Huntsville, Utah, in a blizzard. His plane was not discovered until five months later, in June 1936. He was not there and was presumed dead somewhere.

Another newspaper article about Stark in the *Weekly Reflex* of January 23, 1936, stated that he was "a nationally known authority on blind flying."

After more than three and a half years, Stark's body was found by a sheepherder. The *Salt Lake Telegram* newspaper of September 22, 1939, carried the headline: "Aviator's Body Rests in S.L." The story referred to Stark as the "ace blind flier of the department of commerce."

A view eastward over Huntsville and Ogden Valley. Howard Stark crashed his airplane in 1936 in the mountains on this horizon. *Lynn Arave photo.*

It was determined that Stark had survived his plane crash but not the winter conditions when trying to reach civilization.

If you conduct a Google search for Howard Stark, the first six full pages of results are all references to the fictional Howard Stark of Marvel comics and movies (including posts that speculate on Marvel bringing the character back to life). Finally, at the top of page 7 of Google search results, there's an article in *Vintage Plane* magazine from May 2002 about this real-life Howard Stark. Its headline is "Howard Stark: The Pioneer Aviator of Instrument Flying."

This article, by John M. Miller, says that Stark was flying a Stinson Model S plane for the U.S. Department of Commerce, headed to the West Coast to instruct other flyers about using instruments in airplanes. Ironically, Stark had never been west before, and his plane and equipment were not designed for the high altitude flying of Utah. The article's author believes Stark made an emergency landing in a snowstorm and froze to death trying to walk to safety in deep snow and minus-twenty-degree temperatures.

In the article, Miller stated that "Howard Stark is really the almost forgotten but true father of today's instrument flying....Howard Stark, Charles A. Lindbergh and Clyde Pangborn are my civilian pilot heroes.... Stark's 1-2-3 system has served as the basis for what we know now as partial-panel flying."

So, there you have it. A snapshot of the real Howard Stark. A first-class pilot, and a civilian one at that—just like the fictional Howard Stark.

The first mention of Howard Stark in Marvel tales was in the Iron Man comics of 1970, decades after the real pilot's demise. Tony Stark and his alter ego, Iron Man, debuted in 1963. Tony's father, Howard, was added seven years later. It seems possible that the Marvel writers who created Howard Stark were oblivious to the real one, since he is rarely mentioned in histories—an unjustly forgotten aviation pioneer.

9

LAYTON'S SNOW HORSE

Pioneer Landmark

lmost every spring, an eye-catching white shape trots into view above the Layton area along Utah's Wasatch Range—a stylized equine created by Nature in the watercourses and ridge lines on the high slopes. It is called the Snow Horse, an ephemeral landmark known to early pioneers, probably since the 1850s, and noticed most years as the winter snows melt around the end of May or early June.

A pioneer legend states that if any part of the Snow Horse is still visible by the Fourth of July, there will be plenty of water in the valley throughout the summer. A variation of that legend advises that tender crops should not be planted until the Snow Horse is clearly spotted on the mountain, because that is a sign there will be no more frost. A more modern variant is that parents don't let their children wear shorts or play in outside water each year until the Snow Horse has been spotted, a confirmation that warm weather has arrived.

The Snow Horse is located at about 8,500 feet above sea level on appropriately named Snow Horse Ridge, just east of the Layton-Kaysville border. Deep ravines along the mountainside, where snow accumulates and remains longer than in surrounding areas, help create the unusual shape. In most years, the horse's legs become thinner and thinner as the winter snow melt away.

The Snow Horse varies its appearance year to year. There was a headless Snow Horse in the spring of 2013. The Snow Horse was a no-show in 2007 and 2015 because of meager snowfall.

The Snow Horse above Layton has been a seasonal landmark since pioneer times. This is how it appeared when a late spring snowstorm covered it on June 13, 2017. *Lynn Arave photo.*

Some believe they can also spot a smaller colt-like shape following the Snow Horse. Others claim a bat-like figure sometimes appears. And just above and to the left of the Snow Horse, a *U* shape appears in the snow, which delights University of Utah fans.

A photograph of the Snow Horse hangs inside Layton City's municipal offices at 437 North Wasatch Drive. And Snow Horse Elementary School in neighboring Kaysville is named after the seasonal landmark, though it is not visible as far south as the school itself.

Other so-called mountain shapes reportedly have been spotted in the North Davis–Weber County area. Some profess to see "7" on the north face of the mouth of Farmington Canyon. A banjo shape can sometimes be discerned in the spring around the mouth of Weber Canyon from the Hooper-Clinton area farther west. Some observers claim to see a Scotsman's smiling face each spring on Ben Lomond—a peak that gets its name from a mountain in Scotland, of course.

A prime location for viewing the Snow Horse is around Layton High School or near Gentile Street in Layton. However, if you know where to look, the figure can even be spotted from as far north and west as Hooper.

To best see the springtime Snow Horse, count two major peaks going north (left) from the Francis Peak radar towers that sit prominently above Utah's Davis County. Then, from that second peak, look down a long slope. It is there that the Snow Horse seasonally resides.

10

BEN LOMOND

Mountain of Dreams

Which is Utah's most famous mountain? Some would nominate Kings Peak, the state's tallest, in the High Uintas. Others might say Mount Timpanogos in the Wasatch Range east of Utah Lake. However, Ben Lomond, north of Ogden is better recognized far and wide.

Ben Lomond, at 9,712-feet above sea level, doesn't rank among the 250 tallest named summits in Utah, though it is a prominent one. It isn't even the tallest in Weber County; nearby Willard Peak is 52 feet higher. However, it is still likely the state's most renowned mountain for a simple reason: the movies.

William Wadsworth Hodkinson opened some of the first motion picture theaters in Ogden and subsequently founded Paramount Pictures Corporation in Los Angeles. Paramount is considered the first nationwide film distributor, as well as a prominent filmmaker—one of the Golden Age's original "Big Five" major movie studios.

In 1914, Hodkinson designed a well-known mountain logo for the company, a symbol that has preceded and sometimes concluded scores of motion pictures in various illustrations for more than a century now.

Hodkinson grew up in Ogden. A "majestic mountain"—Ben Lomond— dominated the northern skyline as viewed from his home, rising a vertical mile above the valley floor.

Although two history books written about the studio, *Paramount Pictures and the People Who Made Them* (1980) and *Mountain of Dreams: The Golden Years of Paramount* (1976), do not directly identify the logo's mountain by name,

Paramount Pictures' founder grew up near Ben Lomond, and his memories of the peak inspired the company's famous logo. *Ray Boren photo.*

Leslie Halliwell, who wrote *Mountain of Dreams*, has said, "The mountain he [Hodkinson] doodled on the back of an envelope was a memory of childhood in his home state of Utah."

There is also said to be a plaque in the Paramount Studios lobby in Los Angeles that confirms the mountain in the movie theater's logo was "inspired from his childhood memories."

While Ben Lomond almost assuredly sparked Hodkinson's concept, there are conflicting tales that challenge the claim. But it is also a good idea to emphasize the word *inspiration*. Paramount's appropriately mountain-dominated logo never was actually Ben Lomond—or any other real mountain. It is a fiction, an illustration and one that has been modified substantially over the decades, from an image with a star-crowned peak to a snowy summit wrapped in clouds.

In fact, other mountains in Utah now look more like the logo than Ben Lomond does. Some views of the Pfeifferhorn (also known as the Little Matterhorn) in the Lone Peak Wilderness area south of Little Cottonwood Canyon, for instance, resemble the modern Paramount logo more than anything else.

According to Audrey Godfrey, a Logan historian who grew up in Weber County (and who also writes commentary for Ogden's *Standard-Examiner*),

Ben Lomond was named by her great-great-grandmother Mary Wilson Montgomery, who thought it reminded her of a favorite craggy mountain in her native Scotland.

Ben Lomond is said to translate from a Gaelic/Brittonic root as "beacon mountain," or peak or hill, and signal beacons (*llumon* in Welsh) were probably lit atop it early in Scotland's history. As a result of these derivations, it is repetitive to add *mountain* or *peak* to its name, for that is what the appellation *ben* means.

Godfrey also likes to quote a North Ogden settler, Nephi James Brown, about Ben Lomond, which is pertinent to Paramount Pictures' use of it: "The everlasting majesty of Ben Lomond to the north with its reflected rays of morning sunrise always inspired me as a boy."

Ben Lomond has proved to be a "mountain of dreams" from the valley and in the movies, but it is just as inspiring if you look down after a hike to the summit.

While there's no definitive record indicating who first climbed the mountain, the lower face of Ben Lomond was mined extensively in the

Taylor Arave has a bird's-eye view from atop Ben Lomond, sitting on a summit marker and register. *Lynn Arave photo.*

nineteenth century. Silver and copper were extracted, and a one-hundred-foot shaft was at one time cut into it. Later, mining was conducted to the northwest, below neighboring Willard Peak.

The first known recorded recreational hike up Ben Lomond was reported in the July 3, 1922 *Standard-Examiner* with the headline "Hikers clumb [*sic*] to top of Ben Lomond." Four men climbed from North Fork on the back side of the mountain. They began their expedition at "Smith's ranch" at 9:00 a.m. and didn't reach the summit until 4:15 p.m., according to the newspaper story, indicating there wasn't much of a trail there in those days. However, the men reported that there was a metal box with a register book on top, so they certainly weren't the first up there. Their downward trek required only three hours.

On August 27, 1922, the *Standard* headline was "Over the Top of Ben Lomond Trip of Thrills." The story called the peak by two nicknames: "Old Baldy" and "Old Ben." The left-hand fork of Willard Canyon was the hiking route this time.

Strangely, the story said a highlight of the hike was the "wild chickens," which were "so thick they almost kick one's hat off, flying overhead." Perhaps they were referring to wild grouse.

Fifteen Boy Scouts of Ogden's Troop No. 20 subsequently hiked Ben Lomond, as reported in the *Standard* of August 13, 1923. They trekked from North Ogden Pass and noted the summer wildflowers blossoming around the peak. The boys "returned the short way down the face of the mountain."

An August 11, 1927 *Standard* story told of a climb to the peak by the Wasatch Mountain Club, an organization that still exists. Ben Lomond was described at that time as topping out at 9,100 feet above sea level and offering remarkable views as far north as Preston, Idaho.

11

OLD EPHRAIM

Legendary Grizzly

The tracking, killing and burial in Logan Canyon of a gigantic grizzly bear known as Old Ephraim—which has become a Utah legend—actually didn't stop the demise of sheep, for which a marauding Eph had been blamed by herders and ranchers.

Indeed, "Raid on Grave of Fallen Monarch Avenged by Bears" was a September 13, 1924 headline in Salt Lake City's *Deseret News*. The story, published just over a year after Old Ephraim was killed, reported ominously that after Logan Boy Scouts raided the gravesite of the famous bear that summer, sheep killings picked up.

"The bears have been worse since the scouts were up here digging in Old Ephraim's grave than they have ever been before we came into this county with sheep," said Frank Clark, who was the one who killed Old Eph on August 21, 1923.

"Contrary to bear habits and former history, the bears have been raiding the herds and killing heavily in the daytime, as well as at night," the *Deseret News* story reported.

Clark said that in just one week during the summer of 1924, he lost ten sheep to bears in the same section of the northern Wasatch Mountains that Old Eph roamed. "It seems that Old Ephraim's followers are still loyal," the 1924 *Deseret News* story concluded.

A scout troop had visited the grave of Old Ephraim in the summer of 1924. The scouts dug up the grave and took bones as souvenirs, and the bear's skull was sent to the Smithsonian Institution, the museum and research

Left: The marker at Old Ephraim's grave dwarfs a young boy. Almost ten feet tall, the monument is about the height of the huge grizzly. *Ray Boren photo.*

Below: The inscription on the Old Ephraim monument was erected by boy scouts in 1966. *Ray Boren photo.*

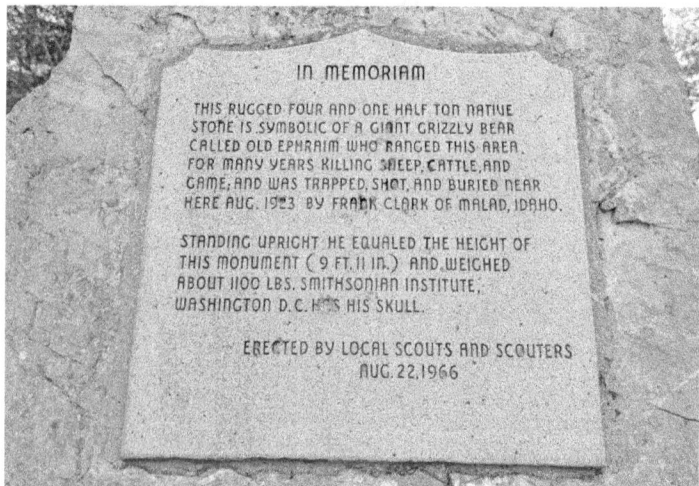

IN MEMORIAM

THIS RUGGED FOUR AND ONE HALF TON NATIVE STONE IS SYMBOLIC OF A GIANT GRIZZLY BEAR CALLED OLD EPHRAIM WHO RANGED THIS AREA FOR MANY YEARS KILLING SHEEP, CATTLE, AND GAME; AND WAS TRAPPED, SHOT, AND BURIED NEAR HERE AUG. 1923 BY FRANK CLARK OF MALAD, IDAHO.

STANDING UPRIGHT HE EQUALED THE HEIGHT OF THIS MONUMENT (9 FT. 11 IN.) AND WEIGHED ABOUT 1100 LBS. SMITHSONIAN INSTITUTE, WASHINGTON D.C. HAS HIS SKULL.

ERECTED BY LOCAL SCOUTS AND SCOUTERS AUG. 22, 1966

organization in Washington, D.C. The skull has since been returned to Utah and is on exhibit at Utah State University.

Old Ephraim was a legendary grizzly bear that roamed the Wasatch in the early twentieth century. Nearly a century after his death, the bruin lives on in campfire tales and tributes.

In a remote side canyon of Logan Canyon, an impressively large stone monument marks where the bear was killed. The 1997 movie *Walking Thunder*, one of actor/singer John Denver's last films, was inspired by the tale of Utah's Old Eph. And in Bear Lake Valley, diners can order an Old Ephraim pizza—thirty-two inches in diameter.

Elusive Eph's demise was big news in 1923. "Grizzly Bear Killed near Logan," Ogden's *Standard-Examiner* announced in a headline on August 22. "The largest grizzly bear that was ever known to inhabit the Wasatch Range is reported to have been killed in the Right Hand Fork of Logan Canyon by William (Frank) Clark, a sheepherder," the story said.

Clark had set many traps for the bear over the years, but the animal evaded them all. Ephraim was finally caught in a trap in the earliest of hours that fateful August morning. However, the bear, reputed to stand nine foot eleven and to weigh some 1,100 pounds, clawed down the eight-inch diameter tree that the trap was tied to and ran up a hill with the trap still on his foot. Clark fired all of his bullets into the bear before Eph dropped.

Years later, Clark reflected on Old Ephraim's end with a *Deseret News* reporter. He said, "I sat down and watched his spirit depart from that great body and it seemed to take a long time, but at last, he raised his head a mite, gasped, and was still. Was I happy? No, and if I had to do it over I wouldn't kill him....I could see the suffering in his eyes as he tried to climb that bank."

Clark claimed to have killed forty-three bears in his thirty-four years of sheepherding, but Old Ephraim was his last, by choice.

Historical accounts describe Eph's range as covering from Weber County, Utah, to Soda Springs, Idaho. But we should include Utah's Morgan County, a little to the southeast, as well, for a November 9, 1911 newspaper story in the *Salt Lake Telegram* reported that a bear-hunting party was looking for Old Eph there too. Led by former Utah governor John C. Cutler, the group spent several days in the wild and found only the bear's huge tracks. Eventually, Ephraim is believed to have settled exclusively in Logan Canyon.

While the bear was originally known as "Old Three Toes" because of a deformity on one foot, showman and entrepreneur P.T. Barnum is said to have affixed the more fanciful name of Old Ephraim to the animal.

The giant bear's legend is concisely summarized in a memorial verse by Nephi J. Bott, inscribed on a plaque at the bottom of the stone monument, erected in 1966 by Logan Boy Scouts, where the bear was buried: "Old Ephraim, Old Ephraim, your deeds were so wrong yet we build you this marker and sing you this song. To the king of the forest so mighty and tall, we salute you, Old Ephraim the king of them all."

12

LEVAN, UTAH

No Navel Here!

I s the Beehive State's most common belly button joke true? Is the name of Levan—in central Utah's Juab County—actually the word *navel* spelled backwards?

That's the crux of a tale passed along for generations, for if Utah had a belly button in its center, Levan would be an ideal candidate. As amusing and widespread as this strange name origin is, it is most likely not true. Yet myth can, and often does, supersede fact over time, and that is almost surely what has happened here.

Consider the following. The first public reference to the town of Levan was possibly in the *Deseret News* on May 6, 1868: "A new town site has been surveyed between [C]hicken and [P]igeon creeks on the east side of the valley some three and half miles northeast of the old Chicken Creek settlement. A field has also been surveyed and improvements have commenced. The new location is called Levan." Some local histories have even referred to Chicken Creek as a previous name of Levan, though the communities were apparently at different sites.

One factor to consider here is that we've got to adjust for history and different borders back then. In 1868, there was no State of Utah—that political designation was twenty-eight years distant. This was the Territory of Utah, and the territory at that time was bigger than the future state, including a portion of western Colorado and a chunk of Wyoming. Thus, the territory was wider in 1868 than today—and if Utah Territory had a "navel," newborn Levan's location wasn't it.

The north entrance to Levan, a town located geographically where a belly button might be—if Utah had a belly button. *Ray Boren photo.*

The central Utah town of Levan is no longer the crossroads it once was, having been bypassed by I-15 since the 1980s. *Ray Boren photo.*

Wyoming was designated a state (taking a northeastern chunk from Utah) three months after the village of Levan got its start, and the State of Colorado came along soon thereafter (taking a far-eastern slice), in 1876. So, Utah's borders didn't assume their present shape until 1876—eight years after Levan came along.

This whittling began long before. The early Mormon settlers first conceived of a "State of Deseret" after their arrival in the region in 1847. In the wake of the Mexican-American War of 1846–48, the settlers had grand, even gigantic, hopes. Their proposed Deseret encompassed much of the Great Basin and even included access to the Pacific, via San Bernardino and San Diego, shortly to become part of California, which became a state startlingly quickly in 1850, after the gold rush of '49. Utah Territory was also organized in 1850. It was still big, encompassing most of Nevada, as well as later parts of Wyoming and Colorado. Nevada was lopped off and became a state of its own in 1864, but even so, Utah Territory retained a portion of today's easternmost Nevada until further boundary changes were made in January 1867.

Pioneer leader Brigham Young is sometimes credited for naming Levan. If so, it probably wasn't because the location was deemed to be Utah's navel. Why in the world would Brigham inaugurate a new town with a jokey name, given the rough living conditions of the time?

In his fascinating book *Utah Place Names*, John W. Van Cott offers this about the Levan's moniker: "There are several French, Latin, or Piute interpretations of the name, suggesting it means East of the Sunrise, Land of the Sunrise, rear rank of a moving Army, Frontier Settlement or Little Water. The tongue-in-cheekers say the name is a reverse spelling of [n]avel, because it is located in the center of the state. Several different spellings have been recorded."

Any of those other meanings makes more sense. Yet ultimately, "Levan-as-Navel" has prevailed because the reference remained undeniably popular.

Even the locals seem to have given in. Former Levan mayor Connie Dubinsky was quoted in the *Salt Lake Tribune* on March 4, 1997, accepting the "navel" origin of the town's name. "We don't really know for sure, but that's what we tell people," she said.

This really is a case of almost universal acceptance of a myth that has become acknowledged as true over time. Levan might not technically be a belly button, but it is undeniably *navel* spelled backward.

And ever since one of the last new sections of Interstate 15 was completed and opened in 1986, the little town needs all the publicity and commerce that it can get. Levan is about eleven miles south of Nephi, along Utah Highway 28. Before 1986, most cross-country traffic headed north or south through Utah went directly through Levan, notably on US 91. Its center still includes a busy convenience store and gas station, but several old-style early twentieth-century filling stations with front porticos line its main thoroughfares. I-15 bypassed Levan completely, US 91 vanished and the little town is not the crossroads it was once upon a time.

13

OAK CITY

Almost Atomic City?

A central Utah town has what might be the greatest "what if?" story to tell in the entire Intermountain region.

An official history of World War II's Manhattan Project reveals an obscure but startling Utah connection—Oak City in Millard County was the search director's first choice for the effort's atomic weapons laboratory. Of course, Los Alamos, New Mexico, eventually won out as the site, but if Oak City had been chosen, it could have significantly altered the Beehive State's history.

Oak City, which has about eight hundred residents, is 125 miles southwest of Salt Lake City and 14 miles east of Delta. Ever been to the Little Sahara sand dunes, a recreation area managed by the Bureau of Land Management? If so, you were just 22 miles north of Oak City.

"That's been well known for years," Kevin Roark, Los Alamos National Laboratory spokesman, said of the town's consideration during the early stage of the Manhattan Project, though he conceded it is an obscure fact. "I don't think the military was keen on Los Alamos," he said.

A fiftieth anniversary article on the history of the Los Alamos National Laboratory notes that Major John Dudley of the Manhattan District Staff was assigned to survey the West and find potential sites for an atomic laboratory in October 1942. The article is posted at on the lab's website. "Dudley searched parts of California, Nevada, Utah, Arizona and New Mexico. His first choice for the laboratory site was Oak City, Utah," according to the Los Alamos history.

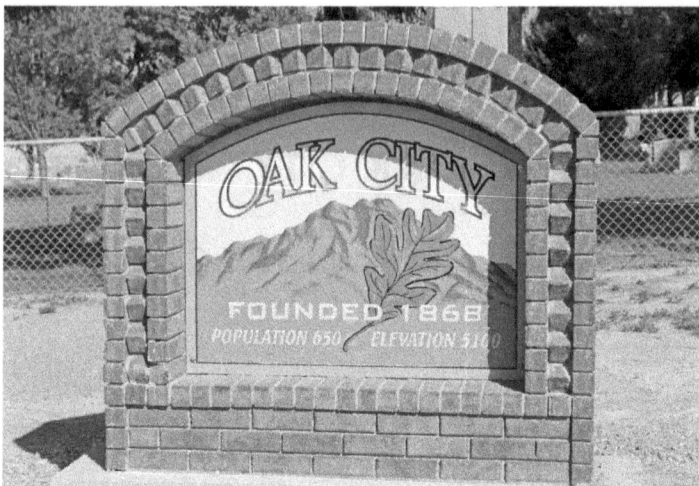

Oak City in Millard County was the search director's first choice for a U.S. atomic weapons laboratory in the early 1940s. *Ray Boren photo.*

"It was a delightful little oasis in south central Utah," Dudley wrote. "The railroad was only 16 miles away over a nice, easy road. The airport was not too distant. The water supply was good. It was surrounded by hills, and beyond there was mostly desert. However, I noticed one thing: If we took over this area we would evict several dozen families and we would also take a large amount of farm acreage out of production."

Because of the potential loss of farmland, Dudley recommended his second choice—Jemez Springs, New Mexico. In the end, Dudley's choice was overruled by J. Robert Oppenheimer, a physicist and the scientific director of the Manhattan Project, who favored Los Alamos.

Roark said that Los Alamos, like Oak City, was inhabited, having a boys school and other residents. Development of the site began in 1943 and worked out well over the years, he said. Outdoor recreation opportunities in the area make it an attractive place to live.

Kent Powell, a Utah State Historical Society historian, said the Oak City connection to the Manhattan Project was news to him. "It is a good 'what if?'" to ponder, he said.

Checking with longtime Oak City residents in 2009, conversations with people between the ages of eighty-two and ninety-five revealed that only one had ever heard about the town being considered for an atomic laboratory. Ava Anderson had read about it in a newspaper article several decades before. She said the matter was so secretive in the 1940s that it was likely no residents knew about it then.

"I hadn't heard that before," said resident Phyllis Anderson, eighty-eight. "We'd have been a lot different place if that had happened." She said she relishes the open spaces of Oak City. She lived in the South for a while and couldn't wait to return to where she was born.

If Oak City had been selected, it might have worked out well. The pilots and crew of the B-29 Enola Gay, which dropped the first atomic bomb on Japan in August 1945, secretly trained just 120 miles to the northwest, in Wendover, Utah.

But the controversies of later atomic testing in Nevada, and its harmful downwind effects on southern Utah residents and beyond, might have started farther north if Oak City had been selected. It's possible that Utah's west desert area or an adjacent part of Nevada might have replaced what is now known as the White Sands Missile Range in New Mexico—about two hundred miles from Los Alamos—as the place where the first-ever atomic bomb was detonated. Had that been the case, more atomic testing might have taken place in or near Utah. On the other hand, the Los Alamos Laboratory has pumped billions of dollars into New Mexico's economy and has provided thousands of jobs for over three-quarters of a century.

14

KANAB ROCKS

Too "Bright" for Hollywood

S outhern Utah is world famous for its colorful landscape. However, there was a time when Hollywood hated the challenging tints of those same canyons, cliffs, buttes and hoodoos.

"Colored rocks of Utah plague film company," declared an October 6, 1940 headline in the *Salt Lake Tribune*. The hues around the Kanab area, in particular, were simply too bright for the technicolor film process Hollywood was using at that time.

"Thousands of tourists visit Utah every year to gaze with wonder and delight at the brilliantly colored rocks dotting the landscape," the story stated. "But these same rocks are a source of annoyance and expense to Twentieth Century-Fox, now on location here for the filming of Zane Grey's 'Western Union.'"

What did Hollywood do? "A crew of men had to be hired to 'redecorate' the rocks along Paris Creek, which cameramen said are too bright for Technicolor filming," the story reported.

The extra cost of the painting before filming was not reported but was believed to be only a small part of the $100,000 (more than $1.8 million in 2021) that the film studio was expected to spend in the Kanab area for the movie. The studio had 470 employees in town for the project, as well as using about 300 Kanab residents as extras, cowpunchers, wranglers and such.

Robert Young, Randolph Scott and Dean Jagger were among the stars in *Western Union*, and the Gap and Johnson Canyon were among the filming locations.

Preparing horses for a movie scene in Universal Pictures' musical *Can't Help Singing* in 1943 near Kanab. *Utah State Historical Society.*

And the tints weren't the only problem Hollywood encountered while filming in the area during the summer of 1940. "While scouting for the Paria [Creek] location, director [Fritz] Lang and his Technicolor staff were marooned when a sudden rain filled the arroyos between Paria and Kanab, blocking their return. They spent the night waiting for the waters to recede while a rescue party tried in vain to reach them," the *Tribune* story reported. This might have been one of the earliest public notices warning that Utah's slot canyons can be dangerous during storms.

Almost exactly ten years later, in 1950, a different Hollywood film crew experienced a similar a red-rock canyon problem. "Mountain 'flash flood' maroons Hollywood Unit," announced an August 12, 1950 headline in the *Ogden Standard-Examiner.*

Buckskin Creek, about forty miles east of Kanab, was struck by a seven-foot-deep deluge, stranding sixty-four members of a filming company for about eight hours. They were making the RKO movie *Best of the Bad Men*, starring Robert Ryan, Jack Buetel, Robert Preston and Walter Brennan in a fictionalized yarn about the Clanton and Younger gangs—the real members of which almost surely never laid eyes on southern Utah's brilliant, and sometimes troublesome, red-rock country.

PART III.

UTAH HIGHS AND LOWS

15

SOUTH KINGS PEAK

Not Utah's Highest

Kings Peak in the High Uintas hasn't always been properly recognized as the "king" of Utah's mountains. The summit now known to be the state's tallest was unacknowledged until the mid-1960s, for another nearby peak was thought to be higher.

Make that peaks, plural.

It took almost 120 years after the arrival of pioneer settlers in the region, and later state, for Utahns—as well as mapmakers and surveyors—to correctly identify and settle on which peak is Utah's tallest. The evolution of thought on the matter has been chronicled in the state's newspapers since the late 1800s, with several candidates being nominated along the way.

According to the *Salt Lake Tribune* of August 18, 1881, Gilbert Peak, also in the Uintas, was first believed to be Utah's tallest, at 13,687 feet above sea level. Kings Peak was not even mentioned then. (And Gilbert is now considered to have an elevation of 13,448 feet.)

By 1903, measurements and determinations hadn't improved much. A *Salt Lake Tribune* article on December 8, 1903, reported that Uintah County surveyors in eastern Utah were claiming that Mount Emmons was the tallest in the state, at 14,449 feet above sea level. (They were just 1,009 feet off the mark. And Utah, it turns out, has no "Fourteeners," sometimes styled "14ers," at all.)

Another newspaper, the *Richfield Reaper*, reported on April 5, 1906, that a Mount Hodges had supposedly been named by U.S. surveyor Clarence King in the 1800s, but no one seemed to know where that peak actually was.

South Kings Peak as it appears from the ridge between it and Kings Peak. South Kings, though sixteen feet shorter, has a wider base. *Lynn Arave photo.*

An April 15, 1911 *Ogden Standard-Examiner* article renominated Emmons Peak (Mount Emmons), at 13,694 feet above sea level, as the tallest. That was the general belief of that year. (And again, the height was not quite right. Today Emmons is deemed Utah's fourth tallest, at 13,448 feet.)

Just two years later, the *Vernal Express* posited in a newspaper story on January 23, 1913, that South Kings Peak was the state's tallest, at 13,498 feet. North Kings, along the same set of ridges, was thought to be second, at 13,496 feet, at the time. The article also indicated that a "South Baldy" and a "North Baldy" were previously thought to be Utah's tallest summits, at 12,210 feet and 12,680 feet, respectively, above sea level.

The *Salt Lake Tribune* of April 10, 1914, finally got it somewhat right. It had Kings Peak as tallest, at 13,498 feet, followed by Mount Emmons, at 13,428 feet, and Gilbert Peak, at 13,422 feet.

Lacking satellite measurements, however, North Kings Peak would not officially, and correctly, be proclaimed highest in the state until 1966. Because of their summit elevations, Kings Peak and South Kings Peak have consistently drawn hikers and mountaineers upward over the years.

The *Roosevelt Standard* newspaper reported on August 20, 1924, that members of the Salt Lake–based Wasatch Mountain Club had hiked Kings Peak (today's South Kings Peak). On top, the members "salted the peak," so to speak, by placing a bottle of briny water from the Great Salt Lake on its lofty summit. The receptacle also had the signatures of Utah governor Charles R. Mabey and others on it.

A 1940s map pegged Kings Peak as the state's tallest, at 13,498 feet above sea level.

A January 30, 1947 newspaper article in the *Vernal Express* reported that in the mid-1940s two men climbed North Kings Peak and constructed a two-foot-high monument on the highest part of the summit, evidently assuming it was that much shorter than South Kings Peak. Then one of the men proclaimed, "There, that makes them even." Other newspapers of the era referred to the "twin Kings Peaks."

For years, that was the accepted belief: South Kings Peak was tallest in the Beehive State. So, anyone hiking Utah's tallest in that time period went to the southern peak—usually missing or bypassing the actual tallest peak, (North) Kings Peak, at 13,528 feet.

In June 1961, a helicopter crash-landed on "Kings Peak." The crewmen walked away unharmed, but the mishap actually took place on today's South Kings Peak. Good thing, too, as South Kings has more usable space on top. Had the crew crashed on today's acknowledged Kings Peak, the copter might have slid hundreds of feet down one steep side or the other.

Lynn Arave looks back toward the rocky slope of Kings Peak, en route to Utah's second-tallest, South Kings Peak. *Courtesy of Roger Arave.*

It wasn't until 1966 that new measurements via satellite determined the northern Kings Peak to be the highest and remeasured South Kings Peak to be second highest. The most recent official federal survey, the North American Vertical Datum of 1988 (NAVD 88), pegs Kings Peak at 13,534 feet in elevation and South Kings Peak at 13,518 feet.

The U.S. Forest Service placed the first official plaque on Kings Peak one year earlier, in 1965. Back then, the Forest Service estimated that only thirty people a year on average hiked to the summit. That has since changed.

Though it is the "monarch" of Utah peaks, Kings Peak is actually named for Clarence King of the U.S. Geological Survey, who explored the Uinta Mountains from 1868 to 1871. He later served as director of the Geological Survey.

By the 1970s, the Forest Service had a metal plaque on the correct tallest Kings Peak. However, that plaque vanished in the late 1990s, presumably removed by vandals who either took it or tossed it off a nearby cliff.

There is a tale that Sir Edmund Hillary, the first to conquer Earth's highest summit, Mount Everest, in 1953, with companion Tensing Norgay, had also climbed Kings Peak. This is actually a true story. It happened in the summer of 1978, when Sears and Kellwood, an outdoor equipment manufacturer, was testing camping gear in the Yellowstone drainage of the High Uintas. Hillary, age fifty-nine by then, was said to have had little trouble hiking Kings Peak and the Uintas.

No stranger to Utah, Hillary backpacked with his family in the High Uintas in the summer of 1962. He also floated the Green River in 1969 as part of the centennial commemoration of the original 1869 exploration of the Green River–Colorado River corridor, led by John Wesley Powell.

Now, in the twenty-first century, dozens of people each summer day are likely hiking to Kings Peak. The most popular starting point is the Henry's Fork trailhead, accessed via seven miles of paved road and almost twenty miles of dirt road from Mountain View, Wyoming. The distance of a roundtrip is thirty miles, with about a 4,130-foot elevation gain. The last mile up Kings Peak is a scramble over large, loose slabs of rock.

By the 1990s, some hikers began taking a steep rockslide "shortcut" that directly accesses Anderson's Pass instead of taking the traditional path over Gunsight Pass and then up Kings Peaks' rocky slope.

Hiking Kings Peak from the trailhead can be accomplished in one long and grueling day, but most conquer it in a two- or three-day backpacking trip, camping at pleasant places like Dollar Lake. At least one Salt Lake group is known to snowshoe or cross-country ski to Kings Peak each winter.

Beyond cliff exposure and such dangers, lightning storms are considered a peril when hiking to, and while atop, Kings Peak.

Though Kings Peak is remote and almost thirty air miles from the nearest town, it has pretty good cell phone reception at the top—though, unsurprisingly, in the surrounding mountain valleys, such service is almost nonexistent.

16

MOUNT NEBO

Wasatch Exclamation Point!

Other peaks along the 250-mile-long Wasatch Range might be more legendary (Mount Timpanogos), more classically elegant (Mount Olympus) and simply more imposing because they loom so dramatically over metropolitan and suburban enclaves (Ben Lomond, Lone Peak), but Mount Nebo—the Wasatch's "final exclamation point in stone," as a writer aptly put it a half-century ago—is actually the highest of them all.

Nebo is actually a triple peak, all three summits aligned atop a dramatic alpine ridge above communities including Mona and Nephi, far below. Nebo's north summit tops out at 11,933 feet above sea level, according to the NAVD 88 survey, but its most-often-accessed South Peak, the second highest, sits at 11,882 feet.

Since the main trails end at South Nebo, most hikers stop there, too— with good reason. After a steep and eventually air-deprived climb to the south peak, it's an additional one-and-a-half-mile scramble, most of it along a precarious knife-edge of rocks, to the higher pinnacle. Those who attempt this adventure get to visit Middle Nebo Peak, as well.

The North Peak is accessed more directly from the Nebo Bench Trailhead, along the Nebo Loop scenic drive or the unpaved Mona Pole Road nearby. The Willow Creek Canyon Trail, beginning on the mountain's western face near Mona, connects with the east-side trail to the South Peak.

The impressive mountain is named for the biblical Mount Nebo in the ancient Mideast region of Moab, near the Dead Sea. The Bible's Book of Deuteronomy says Moses ascended that Nebo "to the top of Pisgah,"

Mount Nebo has three primary peaks. Some trails lead only to the south summit, requiring a knife-edge scramble to reach the middle peak and tallest north peak. *Ray Boren photo.*

from which he observed the Israelites' promised land below before dying and being buried. (In Mormon belief, Moses was "translated" and taken to heaven.)

The biblical Nebo is part of the Pisgah Mountains, east of the north end of the Dead Sea. It is the second-highest peak in the Dead Sea area—2,631 feet above sea level—behind Mount Shihan, at 3,494 feet. However, because the Dead Sea is 1,312 feet below sea level, the Middle Eastern Nebo's climb is more like 3,943 feet, which would be just over half of the Utah Nebo's vertical rise.

The highest summit of Utah's Mount Nebo was "discovered" in the late 1870s, when new measurements were made by the Utah Geological and Mineral Survey. A proposal was made to christen this previously unnamed northern high point "Mona Peak" in honor of the community at the foot of the mountain's western alluvial fan. However, the Utah Committee on Geographic Names decided that the entire mountain had been known for too long as just Nebo, so North, Middle and South Nebo peaks are the specific references now found on any up-to-date map or hiking book.

William W. Phelps, a pioneer songwriter and editor, was the first known person to climb this Mount Nebo, on August 24, 1849, about twenty-five months after the first Mormons arrived in the area, according to the *Garfield*

County News of September 4, 1936. Phelps scaled the mountain for scientific observations, the newspaper says. It is not clear which of the three Nebo Peaks Phelps climbed, nor which route he used to access the summit—if that was even his goal.

"Rearing its majestic peak 12,000 feet above sea level, towering Mount Nebo commands the entire scenic panorama of Juab and adjoining Sanpete Counties," the story's writer observed. "The towering grandeur of this massive peak represents one of Utah's greatest scenic assets."

Phelps's accomplishment was merely the first of many recorded excursions to Nebo's summit. Thomas Moran, a British American landscape artist, used watercolor and pencil on paper for his small work, *Our Camp at Mount Nebo*, inspired by an 1873 trek to the top he made with others while visiting Utah. At the time, Moran—most famous for his artwork depicting the wonders of Yellowstone and the Grand Canyon— thought Nebo to be the "highest mountain in Utah or Nevada," for Utah's Kings Peak had not yet been named or measured. In a letter home, Moran wrote that the view from Mount Nebo "was the most magnificent sight of my life"—high praise considering the amazing Western scenery he had already explored and painted.

The *Deseret News* of August 3, 1887, records another early expedition. On that occasion, a party of seven men left Mona, near the mountain's western base, on July 22 on horseback and rode a narrow course up Willow Creek, or Mona Canyon.

The party stopped and camped that night partway up. They had noticed it was much farther to the summit than they initially believed. Their accounts told of "precipitous ledges" and a "cold wind" over snowbanks, amid the "witches' rocks" and "fields of broken, shifting slate."

They achieved the summit the next day, and a government surveyor, William Elmbeck, used a large telescope to survey the vast expanse below in all directions. Elmbeck estimated the elevation to be 11,943 feet and noted that one of the other peaks was some thirty feet taller, which suggests that they climbed the South Peak.

"Altogether, Mount Nebo is not difficult of ascent, but it is not safe to those unaccustomed to the saddle, and far too rough and hazardous for ladies. Our train of seven horsemen made a pretty sight along a steep serpentine, down which some of the Nephi horsemen occasionally rode at break-neck speed," the article concluded.

That 1887 hiking group was oblivious to the fact that a young lady, a "Miss Bardwell," had successfully climbed Mount Nebo in the summer of 1881,

Ravell Call enjoys the panoramic view atop Mount Nebo's south peak. Note the middle and north peaks rise nearby. *Ray Boren photo.*

according to the *Salt Lake Tribune* of August 18, 1881. The *Tribune* referred to her climb as "a great feat" and reported that she might have done it alone.

The *Deseret News* of June 18, 1898, reported a climb of Mount Nebo's North Peak by a Salt Lake City Sunday school teacher, E.G. Rognon, and five male class members. They erected an 8-foot-tall wooden pole on the peak. They thought this was significant, since government surveyors then believed incorrectly that the peak was 11,992 feet above sea level, and their stunt made it an even 12,000. The group also put their names in a tin can and left it on the summit.

Mount Nebo's hiking heyday came soon after. On March 1, 1920, the *Salt Lake Herald* headlined a story "Aloft on Mount Nebo; Utah Peak Has Beauty of Alps; Grandeur in View." By then, a "safe trail" to the summit had been made from Salt Creek, a much-used path even today. The trail was constructed in 1919, and eighty-two people climbed to the summit on August 6, 1919, the start of an annual mass group pilgrimage to Mount Nebo's top. An estimated three thousand people in the summer of 1919 enjoyed camping on the east side of Mount Nebo in the Salt Creek area.

Nebo was mentioned in the *Salt Lake Telegram* newspaper of March 25, 1920, as a candidate for an observatory atop its summit. This was to be a "Yankee Memorial," to honor the soldiers, sailors and marines of all wars that the United States had been involved in.

The *Telegram* also suggested that a radio broadcast facility—radio was a novel and expanding medium one hundred years ago—could be housed on Nebo's lofty summit. Another proposal recommended setting up a searchlight on Nebo, perhaps to be powered by the streams around the huge mountain.

The *Manti Messenger* reported in a newspaper story on July 31, 1925, that the Kiwanis Club of Nephi was a sponsor of an annual hike up Mount Nebo. The mass trek was held on August 5 that year, under a full moon so that hikers could enjoy the sunrise at the summit.

The Salt Creek trail to Mount Nebo was referred to as the "trail of a thousand turns." The story also referred to Nebo as a "solitary sentinel of the southern Wasatch."

"Gov. [George] Dern Leads Party to the Top of Mount Nebo," read an August 19, 1927 headline in the *Mount Pleasant Pyramid*. The state's governor and many others witnessed the sunrise while on top of the lofty peak. Later that day, there was a program with speeches and a performance by the Nephi High School Band. At evening time, a large bonfire was lit.

On July 4, 1930, Harrison R. Merrill, a *Deseret News* reporter, joined thirty-three Brigham Young University students and faculty members on a Nebo hike and then a nine-mile trek to Nebo's southern summit. Merrill noted how much drier the terrain was along the Nebo route compared to Timpanogos' water-blessed trails. That is, until a big rainstorm hit and drenched the hikers. The group also reported seeing elk.

Twenty-seven hikers reached the summit, and Merrill described his feelings while on top: "Eleven-thousand feet above sea level, like specks along the ridge pole of the world, we sat down and feasted," he wrote. "While our eyes gorged, we ate our lunches beside a little fire that sent its pinion pine smoke toward heaven. It was a huge altar....Cold, austere, a triple pyramid of limestone, Mount Nebo rises under the central Utah sky, the final exclamation point in stone of the Wasatch Mountains."

The annual hike up Mount Nebo seems to have continued for some years. It likely died out for the same reasons that doomed an even more popular annual summer hike up Mount Timpanogos—too many people on the mountain at once for proper safety and conservation.

In the summer of 1933, a Civilian Conservation Corps (CCC) camp was established in the area of Mount Nebo. That crew began construction on the scenic loop road that goes around the back of the peak between Payson and Nephi.

Mount Nebo's name fits in well with the many other biblically tagged communities in the vicinity—Jericho, Ephraim, Goshen and Abraham among them. Settlers obviously liked to apply references to their scriptures. Book of Mormon names were also popular in central Utah, from Deseret and Lehi to Manti and Moroni.

Perhaps the Mormon settlers who caught sight of and named Mount Nebo in the late 1840s realized the big mountain had a fine view of their promised land—much like the one Moses had thousands of years before.

17

LA SAL MOUNTAINS

Balcony of the Beehive State

I f the soaring Uinta Mountains are the "roof" of Utah, then the La Sal Mountains, east of Moab, might be the "balcony" of the Beehive State. Straddling Grand and San Juan Counties near the Colorado border, this king-size mountain range is a snow-capped sky island for most of the year, offering a sharp contrast to the red-rock landscapes of nearby Arches and Canyonlands National Parks.

The La Sals boast Utah's eight tallest peaks outside of the High Uintas and include a dozen summits more than 12,000 feet above sea level. The high point of the La Sals is Mount Peale, at 12,726 feet, according to the NAVD 88 survey. Other than here and in the High Uintas, there are only two other places in Utah—along the Beaver/Piute County line and in western Juab County—where elevations top the 12,000-foot mark.

Salt Lake County's tallest summit, American Fork Twin Peaks, is 11,489, more than 1,200 feet shorter than the high point of the La Sals. Even Utah County's highest point, North Nebo, at 11,933 feet above sea level, is more than 700 feet lower than Mount Peale.

In addition, while the High Uintas are more like a high plateau, the La Sals are mammoth mountains towering over Moab below. The vertical elevation difference from Kings Peak to its adjacent valley is just 2,728 feet, but for Mount Peale, the elevation drop to Moab is more than triple that, at about 8,720 feet, making it Utah's biggest differential in that category.

"They're an island in a sea of desert," Glenn Casamassa, Moab/Monticello district forest ranger, says. "They're one of the most photographed mountain

Utah Highs and Lows

The La Sal Mountains, snowcapped much of the year, soar to almost thirteen thousand feet in elevation. They tower over the area southeast of Moab and Arches National Park. *Ray Boren photo.*

ranges in the world." He said the La Sals and their closest cousins, the peaks of the Abajo Range forty miles to the southwest, are unlike anything else in Utah and more like Colorado's San Juan Range.

From the national parks below, Casamassa said, the La Sals, a part of the Manti–La Sal National Forest, offer an incredible backdrop—and a sharp contrast to the nearby red-rock country. "They're unique and a different eco-system from the red rock," he said. They even host a few unique plants, such as the La Sal daisy, found nowhere else in the world.

Tourists do comment on the La Sals' beauty and vistas, Casamassa says. But he acknowledges that the mountains are often overlooked by some casual visitors, deemed nothing more than a sideshow to the national parks. "People do look to the parks," he said.

For local residents, however, the La Sals are an oasis where they can escape one-hundred-degree-plus summer heat. Temperatures in the mountains, by contrast, tend to peak seventies in summer. Moab's newspaper, the *Times Independent*, reported in its July 20, 1900 edition that Moab residents were heading up in the mountains to escape the summer heat. At least fifty people had headed for the hills to enjoy the mountain air. The main activities on this occasion included dancing, singing and eating.

One of the best sources for information about the range is *La Sal Mountains Hiking and Nature Handbook* (Canyon Country Publications), a 1995 book by Jose Knighton. He eloquently describes the La Sals as "a displaced hunk of the Rocky Mountains stranded amid the Colorado Plateau's high desert, a biological island."

Casamassa said the La Sals are also a critical watershed for the area, its streams recharging underground water for Moab. "Their water is very valuable, and it's high quality," he said.

A much closer look at the mountains is afforded by the sixty-five-mile La Sal Mountain loop road. The route, almost entirely paved, begins south of Moab and connects on the north, through Castle Valley, with Utah Highway 128, a scenic byway that follows the Colorado River. The La Sal loop road is closed in winter but is usually open March through November. Casamassa said that only a small portion of the road is unpaved, a gravel segment easily negotiated by cars.

This La Sal loop road also provides access to many dirt roads and trails through the La Sal Mountains. Some of these mountain roads are not clear of snow until mid-July, though. Gravel roads leading off the loop connect with the 8,800-foot elevation Oowah Lake campground and the 9,400-foot Warner Campground, as well as other sites.

The general hiking season in the La Sals is Memorial Day to late October, but many consider August and September to be the best months for exploring the highest peaks.

Knighton describes the La Sals as having a "maze of unmarked trailheads."

Indeed, Casamassa said the La Sals are still an uncrowded place to escape civilization and exploring them can require a bit of trailblazing. There is no trail to the top of Mount Peale, for instance, so hikers should consult a hiking guide or the U.S. Forest Service for information. At best, the hike to Peale is a difficult five-mile roundtrip that climbs more than one thousand feet per mile. The hike begins at La Sal Pass, north of Medicine Lakes, where the elevation is already over ten thousand feet.

The first recorded hike up Mount Peale was reported in the *Salt Lake Tribune* of September 3, 1937. Members of the Wasatch Mountain Club had a two-day hiking trip there over Labor Dy weekend.

One might assume that the history-making Dominguez-Escalante expedition of 1776 offered the first non–Native American look at the La Sal Mountains. The party, led by two Spanish priests, was trying to find a route to link Santa Fe with mission settlements nearby in California. And while the expedition did pass by the peaks (and even named them—Utah's "La

The La Sal Mountains, Utah's second-highest range, provide a dramatic backdrop to Arches National Park. *Ray Boren photo.*

Sals" are the "Salt" Mountains), writer Jose Knighton believes there is good evidence they were actually viewed eleven years earlier.

In 1765, Juan Maria Antonio de Rivera passed by the La Sals and entered Castle Valley, northeast of Moab. A Spanish explorer in search of gold, Antonio supposedly went through the area on the advice of an Indian guide. The name *La Sal* is usually attributed to Fray Silvestre Velez de Escalante. He thought the white on top of the mountains in mid-summer was salt and not snow. After all, this is a desert. Indians had also previously shown explorers salt deposits at the base of the mountains.

For Ute Indians, the La Sals were likely a prime hunting area, as well as a retreat from the summer. However, bighorn sheep, grizzly bears and wolves had been exterminated in the range by the early 1900s. There are also no moose today. But there are black bears, bobcats, cougars, deer, foxes, raccoons and other small mammals.

Mormon settlers entered the Moab area in 1855. But less than a year later, they were chased out by the Utes. Two settlers among the original forty-four were killed by the Indians. The pioneers called the range the Elk Mountains, oblivious to the Spanish name.

Explorer and geologist John Wesley Powell saw the La Sal Mountains from a distance during his 1869 and 1871 journeys through the region, exploring the Green River and Colorado River canyons.

The mountains were officially renamed La Sal during an 1875 geographic survey of the Four Corners area headed by Ferdinand Vandeveer Hayden. The government survey crew was attacked by Indians. There was no loss of life, but some of their equipment had to be abandoned during the chase.

Several of the peaks were also named at this time. Mount Peale was named for Dr. Albert Peale, a mineralogist during the Hayden Survey. Although Peale is the tallest, it is not the most dominant peak for onlookers. The summit is set back far enough to the east—1.5 miles behind 12,482-foot-high Mount Tukuhnikivatz (say "Tuk-a-nik-ivatz")—that it hardly stands out. "Tuk" and Mount Mellenthin (elevation 12,645) are generally the most striking La Sal peaks.

Ute Indians are said to have named Tukuhnikivatz for "a place where the sun sets last" or "where the sun lingers." Another legend relates that the peak was named after a Ute medicine man and translates roughly as "dirt seer."

Tuk is noticeable because its southern flank has a long slope that drops down like a huge slide.

Mellenthin (pronounced "Melon-teen") was named for Rudolph E. Mellenthin, a forest ranger in the area who was shot and killed while attempting to apprehend a World War I draft dodger on August 23, 1918. Another lofty peak, Mount Waas (12,331), was named by the Hayden survey for a local Ute Indian chief.

Cowboys and cattlemen were prominent among those who came to permanently settle at the base of the La Sals in 1877.

There was a gold rush in the area during 1888, when the precious metal was found on the slopes of Mounts Waas and Green. This led to a town in Miner's Basin at the ten-thousand-foot level, complete with a store, saloon and several restaurants. It was a ghost town by the early 1900s, when the gold gave out.

The La Sals' Gold Basin, another mining site, below and west of Mount Mellenthin, has a similar story. An advertisement appeared in the *Times Independent* edition of August 3, 1900, with the declaration, "Wanted—1000 prospectors in the La Sal Mts." Gold was advertised as being prevalent in the quartz common in the mountains. It was an attempt to restart the mining boom.

Some of today's roads through the La Sals probably had their beginnings in the miners' days. A Civilian Conservation Corps workforce of some two hundred men in 1933 improved many roads and trails through the area, benefitting those exploring the "salty" mountains to this day.

18

BEEHIVE PEAK

A Red Pyramid

A s seen from the valley below, a prominent summit on the edge of central Utah's Pahvant Plateau looks like the state symbol—a beehive. But while Beehive Peak, west of Aurora, could conceivably be a candidate for the state's official mountain, from another angle, it summons up a different locale: Egypt. From vantages three thousand feet higher, on the plateau's rugged roads, Beehive Peak looks like a mysterious—possibly even manmade—red pyramid.

The peak, in Fishlake National Forest, is a prominent landmark for much of Sevier County, especially the communities of Aurora, Salina and Redmond. Its two faces make the mountain one of Utah's most unusual, though it isn't listed on the state highway map.

"It just stands out," says Bill Wright, a ranger with the forest's Fillmore District. "It's a nice red in color."

Max Reed, a ranger in the Fishlake National Forest, would agree. "It's really quite pretty when the sun hits it," he said.

"For me it's security," said Richard Wasden, a rancher who has cattle each summer in the Beehive Peak area. "You wake up and there it is." He uses it as a landmark to know where he is on the mountainous plateau.

The "distinctive pyramid of Beehive Peak" is how Peter Massey and Jeanne Wilson describe it in their book, *4WD Adventures Utah*.

Although the Willow Creek Road/Piute ATV Trail, usually open late June through October, comes within about three miles of the mountain, there is no developed trail to the peak itself. Those interested in getting to it

Beehive Peak resembles an Egyptian pyramid from the lofty Pahvant Mountain plateau.
Lynn Arave photo.

have to bushwhack and maneuver through a maze of cow trails, ridge lines and scree to its base.

Once there, layers of a sheer "China wall" circle the summit. The rugged formation is also composed of a brittle sandstone material that makes it extremely difficult—as well as dangerous—to climb. Trees growing on the peak's sides make it appear climbable from a distance, but close-up the spot has a rugged Bryce Canyon look. Still, daring hikers have conquered not only the protective walls but also Beehive Peak itself.

The first recorded climb to Beehive Peak was reported in the *Salt Lake Herald* of August 25, 1901. T.E. Newman and Mr. Woodbury were said to have made the climb up and back in five hours.

Steve Camp of Salina was another successful climber in more recent decades. "I was surprised at how difficult it was" because of the steepness and the loose, brittle rock, he said. Camp found a crack in the natural walls around the summit's southwest side and reached the pyramid's base. He made his final approach up the peak on the northwest side. "There were some cliffs to shimmy up."

Camp has since met a few others who have reached the top, and they agree Camp's route is the best approach. It's such a magnificent landmark that—having grown up in the area—he said he had to try to climb it. And he would like to do so again.

The red rock that composes Beehive Peak is believed to be material shed from an ancient mountain range that preceded the Pahvant Range. Camp said nearby Red Canyon also contains interesting rock formations.

Beehive is overshadowed in height by four other peaks nearby—Jack's Peak (10,072 feet), White Pine Peak (10,215), Coffee Peak (10,005) and Willow Creek (9,765). However, like some Egyptian monoliths, it is Beehive's shape that startles and attracts. Also, "It's further east than the rest of the higher peaks," Wright said, and therefore more prominent to those in the valley below.

Surrounded by three deep canyons—Sweetwater, Red and North Cedar Ridge—Beehive Peak can also be spotted along the eastern end of US 50, between Scipio and Salina, and along portions of US 89 and I-70.

Closest access to the peak is the Willow Creek Road, a truck, four-wheel-drive or ATV dirt highway also known as US Forest Road No. 102. Access is also possible from Richfield on a dirt road past the Redview Guard Station on Forest Road No. 96 that connects with the Willow Creek Road.

Beehive Peak does indeed look like a gigantic beehive from the Sevier Valley below. *Ray Boren photo.*

Mount Nebo is visible to the north from near and atop the Pahvant Plateau. Mary's Nipple is the most prominent peak to the east across the Sevier Valley. The Tushar Mountains can be spotted to the south. Fall leaves also make the Willow Canyon area a spectacular drive in autumn.

19

NOTCH PEAK

Acrophobic Nightmare

Western Utah's Notch Peak is a true test for those with acrophobia. It is, quite simply, the state's ultimate drop-off. Glance (carefully) over its northwest edge from the top and it is a three-thousand-foot drop with another two thousand feet of gradual slope down to Tule Valley to the west. The cliffs rival those in Yosemite National Park, climbers say, making Notch a dream spot for hang gliders and BASE jumpers.

The five-mile trek to the top of Notch Peak, fifty miles southwest of Delta, at first follows a narrow canyon. There is a 3,225-foot elevation gain to reach the 9,655-foot peak of this distinctively shaped mountain. The refreshing solitude along the way and at the top is another plus of this remote hike.

The summit of Sawtooth Mountain in Utah's House Range, Notch Peak has had its own "mailbox" in the past, one of those familiar general-issue tin versions, embedded in an impressive rock cairn. David G. rhapsodized in the register found therein: "It's not heaven, but you can see it from here."

Carl B. took in the view and then decided to "sit back, close my eyes and imagine Lake Bonneville filled to the brim."

According to an inscription in the notebook, the mailbox was first placed there by the Wasatch Mountain Club in 1968. So shiny it looks nearly new, the box is often stuffed with notes left by hikers—Scout troops, people in pairs and small groups—who reached the peak.

Judging from the register, Notch seems to give just about everyone a tingle of acrophobia.

"Wow! Dang," Erick, Lisa and Sue succinctly exclaimed.

"It gives me the heebie jeebies," an unknown scribe noted.

Above: An eastern view of the House Range's Notch Peak, highlighting its defining characteristic. The birds are migrating snow geese. *Ray Boren photo.*

Opposite: The sheer northern face of Notch Peak, with the Tule Valley below. *Lynn Arave photo.*

Sheer, steep, lofty, abrupt—adjectives don't do this escarpment justice.

John Hart, in his book *Hiking the Great Basin*, writes that a Notch Peak climb will refine your use of the word *cliff*. It is, he says, "the ultimate drop-off." Perhaps only El Capitan in Yosemite is a worthy rival of Notch Peak in terms of sheer cliff-ness.

A hike to the top begins at the mouth of Sawtooth Canyon on the mountain's southeast side. A shot-up sign meant to direct motorists to nearby Miller Canyon (the placard on the main unpaved road heading north says "er Canyon") sends adventurers west; at a Y intersection, the road on the right heads to Miller, while the one on the left bumps toward Sawtooth.

Finally, hikers head up a ridge toward the peak. Before they get there, though, the mountain suddenly breaks open and YIKES! A massive cleft opens up, a yaw that certainly contributes to the notch visible from scores of miles away. The mountain's limestone foundations swirl in a sequence of sedimentary layers.

From the peak itself, Notch, at 9,655 feet above sea level, drops 5,053 vertical feet on its west side to the bleak but beautiful sagebrush-and-alkali Tule Valley below. That, as Fergus points out, is nigh on a mile.

Notch Peak from the west, showcasing a vertical drop second to none in the Intermountain West. *Ray Boren photo*.

Then there's the view from the top: a panorama of desert valleys and distant ranges. On a clear day, there are more sights to behold than you might have time to drink in. "Scenic overdose," two Provo hikers scribbled in a mailbox note.

Notch Peak has been a landmark around the Delta area and the west desert for centuries. However, when was it first climbed? The earliest account available is from April 19, 1930, when four men—Blaine Cropper, Ellis Bennett, Lester Cropper and Wallace Nilson—scaled its summit and left their names behind on a weathered piece of paper inside a stone pile on the summit. These names were rediscovered more than eight years later on August 20, 1938, when J.H. Belt of Salt Lake City climbed to the top of Notch Peak.

The name of another peak bagger, Louis Schoenbergerm, from May 25, 1930, was also written on the aged paper.

As reported in the *Millard County Chronicle* of August 25, 1938, Belt was stunned by the beauty of the area. He said he could clearly see Mount Nebo, Mount Timpanogos and even some Nevada summits from Notch Peak. "On top I found a stupendous sight," Belt told the newspaper. "Peak after peak arises in majesty across a vista of many miles."

20

BEAVER DAM WASH

Utah's Basement

U tah prides itself on enjoying and promoting "Life Elevated"—a state slogan. Indeed, Utah has some of the highest average elevations of any state in the union. As previously mentioned, the Beehive State's highest point is Kings Peak, at 13,534 feet above sea level, in the Uinta Mountains.

But what is the lowest point in Utah?

It might be surprising to some to learn that it is not St. George. The lowest altitude is, however, in that southwestern corner of the state.

Travel some 325 air miles straight southwest from Kings Peak, ultimately drop some 11,350 feet in elevation (about 2.15 miles), and you reach Beaver Dam Wash at the Utah-Arizona border. That's the state's basement, at 2,178 feet above sea level. For comparison, St. George sits at 2,800 feet, and Salt Lake City's Temple Square is at 4,327 feet above sea level.

Just like Kings Peak, there are no cities or residences in the immediate vicinity of Utah's portion of Beaver Dam Wash. This is open wilderness. Littlefield, Arizona, is the nearest town, about ten air miles away, while St. George is almost twenty-five miles away, as the bird flies. There is a ranch about six miles north, but that's it—at least as far as humans are concerned. Range cattle nibble what they can in places. And the wash is recognized for a variety of wildlife—desert plants, birds, lizards and mammals.

Before 2006, the majority of sources out there—including books and the internet—listed Utah's lowest elevation incorrectly. Some indicated the low point was 2,350 feet above sea level, while others had it at an even 2,000 feet. The truth is about halfway between those numbers.

The left side of this picture (and of the fence line) is where Utah's lowest elevation can be found, in Beaver Dam Wash. *Lynn Arave photo.*

On June 6, 2006, three *Deseret News* staff members—this book's co-authors, Lynn Arave and Ray Boren, and their friend Ravell Call—searched the area with a GPS device and came up with the now-accepted low altitude elevation at the state line: 2,178 feet.

To reach the lowest point in the state, the trio drove five miles along a rugged dirt road off Old US 91 and then hiked two miles over trail-less terrain to the Arizona-Utah border, marked with a wire fence. From the Utah side of the line, they took dozens of measurements with a GPS in various low points until the lowest number was found and verified.

Not only is the Beaver Dam Wash Utah's lowest place, but it is also part of an ecosystem unlike anything else in the state. It is in the Mojave Desert, where Joshua trees, yucca, blackbrush, creosote and other desert plants thrive in a usually dry and scorching environment.

The *Deseret News* consulted with Mark Eubank, chief meteorologist of Salt Lake City's KSL-TV, Channel 5, at the time. "In general, the lower the elevation, the hotter the temperature," Eubank said. "That is why Death Valley is the hottest place in North America—elevation near 200 feet below sea level. There are no official temperature readings from Beaver Dam Wash, but I feel certain it averages hotter there than in St. George."

Eubank noted that Mesquite, Nevada, southwest of Beaver Dam Wash, runs two to five degrees hotter than St. George most days.

Chris Gibson, a meteorologist with the Salt Lake Office of the National Weather Service, agreed. Beaver Dam Wash "probably is the hottest place in Utah," he said. Temperatures usually drop 5.5 degrees Celsius for every one thousand feet of altitude descended. On a hot, still day, Gibson believes Utah's lowest point would be at least a couple of degrees warmer than St. George.

June 6, 2006, was a sunny, hot day. Mesquite reached 106 degrees. By late morning in the Beaver Dam Wash, temperatures were already in the upper nineties. One of the group's thermometers measured 110 degrees as they headed back to their vehicle.

While getting lost in the wash is unlikely, especially since power transmission lines go through the area and following them south would lead to the dirt road, there was no trail. Following one's footsteps back was next to impossible. A shortcut through heavy brush got you somewhat out

This black GPS device identified Utah's lowest elevation, 2,178 feet above sea level, in 2006. The fence marks the Utah-Arizona border. *Lynn Arave photo.*

of the sun but slowed the trek significantly and required some zigzagging and bushwhacking.

While Beaver Dam Wash is up to a half-mile wide in spots, loose sand and gravel, marshes and thick brush make walking difficult.

The 2,178-foot altitude measure has become the accepted standard for Utah's lowest elevation. It is now listed not only on the official Utah highway map, but it has also been highlighted in a high/low comparison in the Natural History Museum Utah at the University of Utah.

How does one know that the elevation the *Deseret News* came up with is accurate?

After returning from their expedition, one of the three hikers consulted with Mark Milligan, a geologist with the Utah Geological Survey. He found on detailed quadrangle maps of the area that the lowest spot in Utah would be bounded by 2,160-foot and 2,180-foot contour lines. "The border is much closer to the 2,180 contour, and thus agrees with an elevation of 2,178 feet," he wrote in an email to the *Deseret News*.

Milligan also indicated that 2,178 is as close an estimate to the low elevation as is possible because the Beaver Dam Wash is prone to flooding, so its elevation can change.

Despite the hot temperatures in the Beaver Dam Wash, it isn't completely waterless. A few springs keep water there year-round. The water runs as a small stream above ground at the end of the dirt road into the Wash. Walking north in the Wash, the water disappears and again goes underground.

To travel to Utah's lowest point, you really need a truck, a four-wheel drive vehicle, an off-road motorcycle, an off-highway vehicle (OHV) or a mountain bike, unless you want to tromp an extra six miles along dirt roads in the desert. The road is simply not passable for regular cars because of several dips in the road that exceed the ground clearance.

Utah's Kings Peak ranks as the seventh highest among high points in the fifty states. For low points in the United States, Beaver Dam Wash ranks fourth among the highest of low points. Only Colorado (3,320 feet), Wyoming (3,099) and New Mexico (2,840) have higher low points. Montana rates fifth place at 1,800 feet.

Of course, for twenty-one coastal states, the lowest elevation is much simpler to figure out.

It is sea level.

PART IV.

UTAH HEAVEN AND HELL

21

ZION CANYON

In Heaven's Name

Zion National Park is without a doubt one of Utah's premier outdoor treasures. Visited by some three million people annually, Zion is steeped in religious overtones beyond its very name, with at least two dozen additional biblical, Book of Mormon and even Native American spiritual names adorning its lovely landscape.

Surprisingly, the city of Ogden, though it is some 350 miles from Zion in northern Utah, has a strong connection to at least two and possibly three of the park's most famous landmarks—the Great White Throne, Angels Landing and the Three Patriarchs: Abraham, Isaac and Jacob.

Frederick Vining Fisher, an Ogden resident and former pastor of the First Methodist Episcopal Church of Ogden, named the three sites during a visit to Zion in 1916, or perhaps even earlier in 1914, as one early Zion National Park brochure from the late 1930s posits.

Fisher, an early non-Mormon apologist, made a trip up Zion Canyon, the heart of today's national park, which was known at the time by a variety of names: Little Zion, the Heavenly City of God or Mukuntuweap, understood to mean "Straight Canyon" to the Southern Paiute Indians. Fisher was accompanied by two locals, Rockville LDS bishop David Hirschi and his son, Claude Hirschi.

The afternoon sun gloriously illuminated the Great White Throne and inspired Fisher to reportedly say, "Never have I seen such a sight before. It is by all odds America's masterpiece. Boys, I have looked for this mountain all my life, but I never expected to find it in this world. This mountain is the Great White Throne."

On an autumn day, the Virgin River rushes toward the Watchman, a prominent mountain above Zion National Park's main south entrance. *Ray Boren photo.*

Dr. Fisher, then going by an educational rather than a religious title, also noticed a large rock formation on the opposite side of the narrow canyon, northwest of the Great White Throne, and once again made a religious connection. He surmised that angels would never land on the nearby Great White Throne—that was a seat for deity—but would instead reverently perch on a nearby footstool to pay their obeisance. Hence, Angels Landing, which is today one of the most popular and exciting hikes in the national park.

The credit for naming the Three Patriarchs is not as definitive. Some accounts say Fisher named it, while others point to Claude Hirschi.

Fisher had lived in Alaska before coming to Ogden, and he had visited other wonders of the West, including Yosemite, Yellowstone and the Grand Canyon. Still, he referred to Zion as a "wonderland of nature" and gave frequent lectures during the 1910s across the nation, highlighting Utah as the "Crown Jewel of the Continent" with its outdoor treasures. Fisher also often spoke in the Ogden LDS Tabernacle and was good friends with David O. McKay, then an apostle in the hierarchy of the Church of Jesus Christ of Latter-day Saints.

Overall, Zion is indeed an unusual national park, one where most visitors are provided with a brief biblical and Book of Mormon education whether they want it or not because of the many religious place-names. Ride the shuttle buses in Zion, and the audio recordings will recite some of this religious history as heavenly landmarks along the way are pointed out.

Local Native Americans had for centuries known of and revered Zion Canyon, which some considered a dark and narrow place they feared to enter. Mormon settler Nephi Johnson is the first non-Indian known to visit Zion Canyon, in 1858.

Another Mormon pioneer, Isaac Behunin, constructed a log cabin at today's Springdale in January 1862. By the summer of 1863, he had built another cabin and farm, this one near where today's Zion Lodge resides. Behunin promoted the name "Little Zion" for the area and supposedly proclaimed, "A man can worship God among these great cathedrals as well as in any man-made church—this is Zion."

Behunin was also reputed to have said, "Why go to Zion [Salt Lake City] and worship in a temple when we have God's own temples here? This is as much Zion as Salt Lake. We'll call it little Zion." Behunin used to sit in front of his cabin and admire the spectacular canyon walls. His name of "Little Zion" took hold for a time.

Zion National Park's Angels Landing (*center*) and Great White Throne beyond. The famed switchbacks of Walter's Wiggles are visible at the bottom. *Lynn Arave photo.*

However, LDS church president Brigham Young, hearing of this, later stressed to early settlers in the Springdale area that the canyon was not Zion, despite their heavenly descriptions. Some of the settlers then began sarcastically calling the area "Not Zion."

Behunin Canyon, northwest of the Emerald Pools, is named in the pioneer's honor.

Joseph S. Black, still another Mormon pioneer, was so excited by Zion Canyon's beauty that he provided what others considered to be unbelievable early descriptions of the place. Some skeptics then sarcastically dubbed the area Joseph's Glory.

The following are some of the other religious names in Zion National Park:

Zion, the park's overall name, of course has roots in both the Bible, as well as in LDS scriptures. *Zion* is a Hebrew word referring to a place of safety or refuge.

Kolob Canyons and Kolob Arch get their titles from the Pearl of Great Price, an LDS book of scripture that mentions a star, Kolob, as the nearest residence of God.

Mount Moroni is named for a Book of Mormon prophet.

Orderville Canyon was named for the town of Orderville, west of Zion along US 89, and the LDS Church's nineteenth-century United Order cooperative plan.

There's also Tabernacle Dome, the Organ (originally the Great Organ), Church Mesa, the North and South Guardian Angels, the Altar of Sacrifice, the Pulpit, Cathedral Mountain and Canaan Mountain.

Explorer John Wesley Powell visited Zion in 1872 and learned of or applied Indian names, such as Mukuntuweap to the North Fork of the Virgin River and Parunuweap (Water that Roars) to the East Fork. Yet even Powell, the scientist, felt spiritual in Zion, since he named the East and West Temples.

The Temple of Sinawava, at the end of Zion Canyon's road and the beginning of the Zion Narrows, was named by Douglas White of the Union Pacific Railroad to honor Sinawava, the Paiute coyote spirit. Mount Kinesava is named for another Paiute deity.

The naming of the Virgin River, which carved Zion Canyon and beyond over the eons as a tributary of the Colorado River, is more of a mystery. The stream might have been named by Spanish explorers or traders in honor of Mary, the mother of Jesus.

But historians say it ultimately might have been named by explorer and cartographer John C. Frémont in the mid-nineteenth century for an early mountain man, Thomas Virgin. Virgin traveled with legendary explorer Jedediah Smith, whose party passed through the area, and along the lower Virgin River, seeking a route to California in 1826.

22

CATHEDRAL VALLEY

Temples of the Sun & Moon

More than two hundred years ago, trappers and other trailblazers pushing into the American West began traversing bleak, torturous landscapes that were mostly barren of vegetation and browse. They called these places badlands. Nowadays, often as not, we call them national parks.

A perfect example can be found in the spectacularly eroded backcountry northeast of Fruita and the Fremont River in south central Utah. There, in 1945, Frank Beckwith and Charles Kelly, the first superintendent of what was then Capitol Reef National Monument, christened an area of fantastically eroded cliffs, sandstone monoliths and panoramic views. To them, the scene seemed downright Gothic.

So, they called it Cathedral Valley. There you'll find, among many other jaw-dropping formations, the Temples of the Sun, Moon and Stars.

This quiet, remote place has a reverent atmosphere filled with solitude and wonder.

"The landscape of South Desert and Cathedral Valley looks eternal," Rose Houk writes in her book *Capitol Reef: Backcountry Eden*. "But change is nature's universal theme."

"It's spectacular and remote," observes Al Hendricks, superintendent of today's Capitol Reef National Park.

Cathedral Valley's sometimes atypical Colorado Plateau scenes are often depicted on postcards and in books but getting there requires heading off the paved U-24 highway that bisects Capitol Reef, often to travel a

The Temple of the Sun, and the smaller Temple of the Moon to the left, are highlights of Capitol Reef National Park's remote Cathedral Valley. *Ray Boren photo.*

dusty—and in wet weather, potentially treacherous—fifty-eight-mile loop that crosses the eerie Bentonite Hills, rises over the South Desert and descends into Cathedral Valley and the Caineville Wash, or vice versa.

Compared to the more popular Waterpocket Fold area to the south, not many people choose to make this trip. "Very often, you may be the only one visiting them that day," Hendricks says.

The Cathedral Valley tour is a fascinating passage through the geologic eons, from ancient seas that laid down sandstone layers to not-quite-so-distant volcanic and ice ages that have left big basaltic boulders strewn about as if giants had been playing marbles with them.

The wonders along this backcountry loop greatly add to Capitol Reef's picturesque inventory. The park's better-known Capitol Dome, Hickman Arch and Grand Wash are familiar to most visitors because of their proximity to historic Fruita, Capitol Reef's headquarters. But the moonscape hills, plateau-top views, shimmering gypsum hillocks and pyramid-like temples in the park's northern sector are certainly worth taking in as well.

Overnight visits are possible, but a minimum of seven hours is usually required to complete the Cathedral Valley loop. The route also passes through some private land, where no trespassing is the rule, and winds in and out of national park boundaries and into Bureau of Land Management territory.

The following are just a few of the sights.

Fremont River Ford: This one obstacle, 11.7 miles east of Capitol Reef's visitor center on the loop's west end, probably deters many a potential backcountry tourist, even though the road beyond is generally OK for all vehicles with good ground clearance. The river crossing is shallow year-round (about ten inches deep), except in spring runoff or after a rainstorm, according to the park's "self-guiding auto tour" tabloid. Access to Cathedral Valley itself is possible at the other end of the loop, at Caineville Wash, 18.6 miles east of the visitor center—and the road there does not require a splash across a river, if you plan on going out the same way you came in.

Bentonite Hills: Their name sounds like a title for a Western novel: "These Bentonite Hills." From a distance, the mounds, about 8.5 miles from the river ford, really do look otherworldly—like an artist's palette, splashed with gray and white and dark vermillion. Up close, the barren soil—"Plants can't take root here," Hendricks says—looks equally alien. Crackly when dry, like stepping on popcorn, it becomes gooey and slippery when wet. So, this part of the loop is best avoided when the latter seems likely.

Cathedral Valley Overlooks: A 1.0-mile hike from the loop road, 17.0 miles from the ford, offers a high view of the Temples of the Sun and the Moon. A spur road 27.2 miles along presents the panorama of Upper Cathedral Valley's monolith complexes.

South Desert Overlooks: There are two major overlooks of the colorful South Desert, one about fourteen miles from the ford, at the end of a short spur (the "Lower" overlook), another atop a high knoll twenty-seven miles along (the "Upper" overlook), near the loop's summit. The views, high on a rising plateau, are to the south toward the Henry Mountains and the Waterpocket Fold, and they are something to behold.

Thousand Lake Mountain: A six-site campground is near the loop's highest point, twenty-eight miles from the river ford, near where a Forest Service road heads off to Thousand Lake Mountain.

Upper Cathedral Valley: Towering above the sloping plain—sometimes five hundred feet tall—the Entrada sandstone monoliths of Upper Cathedral Valley, thirty miles from the ford, rise in spectacular groupings above cracked-mud draws and pinyon-and-juniper lowlands.

Morrell Cabin: Mostly hidden by a small bluff in Upper Cathedral Valley but near the loop road, the Morrell Cabin was used by stockmen and today remembers the park's cowboy past. It was built in the 1920s by a ranching family.

Gypsum Sinkhole: A gigantic cliffside maw opens up below some cliffs at the end of a short spur road thirty-three miles from the ford. Underground

A close look at the Capitol Reef's Temple of the Moon reveals intricate geologic layering and long-term weathering. *Ray Boren photo.*

gypsum deposits have eroded away, creating a sinkhole some two hundred feet deep in places.

Glass Mountain: A shimmering mound off the Lower Cathedral Valley spur to the Temples of the Sun and Moon, 42.5 miles from the river ford (15.5 miles from the Caineville Wash intersection), has been dubbed Glass Mountain. It is specked with unusually large, flat selenite gypsum crystals, also known as moonstone, according to the Park Service. The glassy rock adds to the unearthly setting when the Temples of the Sun and Moon are glimpsed in the near distance.

Temples of the Moon and Sun: This is an intimate "Monument Valley," a place where you can drive right up, touch and ponder layered pyramids in relative solitude. They offer a serene experience that's rare in today's overused national parks. The near-twins stand like sentinels, rising up to four hundred feet high above the valley floor, but visitors can see other incipient temples along the cliffs nearby—the Temples of the Stars.

Spring and fall are Cathedral Valley's busiest periods, according to Hendricks. Summer, he says, is too hot for most visitors.

If there's a catch to Cathedral Valley, it's that it requires that minimum fifteen-mile, one-way drive along Caineville Wash's dirt roads to visit the magnetic Temples of the Sun and Moon. "Our biggest issue here is flashfloods," Hendricks said. He said the valley and the loop drive that accesses it are places where extra water and provisions are wise, because even the park rangers don't travel the road every day—and some days no one might come along to help a stranded traveler.

High-clearance two-wheel drive vehicles can sometimes travel the road safely if some maintenance work has been done. "Four-wheel drive does come in handy here," Hendricks says. He believes deep pockets of dust are a particular hazard currently for two-wheel vehicles. "It's so dry. It's like driving in powdered sugar," he said.

23

THE GREAT STONE FACE

Religious Icon

D oes a likeness of Joseph Smith Jr., first president of the Church of Jesus Christ of Latter-day Saints, exist in the vast Millard County desert, southwest of Delta?

Some believe so.

On a remote hillside in Utah's Sevier Desert, about four miles southwest of the little community of Deseret and some seventeen miles southwest of Delta, rises a craggy volcanic outcrop. For almost seven decades, area residents and visitors have been attracted to the formation. In it, they can discern the outlines of a man's features: head, brow, nose, mouth and even perhaps a high collar.

Welcome to the Great Stone Face or the Guardian of Deseret or the Keeper of the Desert. From a certain angle, notes the book *A History of Millard County*, a 1999 entry in the Utah Centennial County History Series, "some see a resemblance to Joseph Smith," who founded the Church of Jesus Christ of Latter-day Saints, also known as the Mormon Church, in 1830. This remains a seldom-visited landmark for Mormons.

The Great Stone Face was originally called Guardian of the Desert by Millard County newspapers during the 1920s, the era when it first claimed local fame as a tourist destination. Part of that reference is to the nearby town of Deseret.

The Great Stone Face formation was reported as early as November 18, 1927, when the *Millard County Chronicle* reported a visit there by local Boy Scouts. Even then, the perceived likeness to Joseph Smith was noted.

The Great Stoneface is a volcanic rock feature. Some visitors believe it resembles Joseph Smith, founder of the Church of Jesus Christ of Latter-day Saints. *Lynn Arave photo.*

A short path leads from a parking lot to the Great Stoneface formation, located southwest of Delta, Utah. *Lynn Arave photo.*

Utah Heaven and Hell

The *Chronicle* reported on April 7, 1938, that sunrise Easter services were held at the Great Stone Face that year by members of the nearby Hinckley and Deseret wards, or congregations, of the LDS Church.

"Many Mormons see an uncanny resemblance of this naturally carved formation to profile pictures of church founder Joseph Smith," Millard County's official tourism site www.millardcounty.com reads.

Whether or not it is partly the power of suggestion, there definitely is a face to be spotted in the rocks—though some might argue about just whose face it is. Visitors have to decide that for themselves at the site, about 150 miles southwest of Salt Lake City.

The rock pillar sits some 150 feet above the Sevier Desert floor amid a field of lava rock and sagebrush, with a view to Notch Peak to the west.

A steep scramble along a four-hundred-yard-long trail takes hikers to the base of the monument over loose rock. A rugged path outlined by lava rocks marks the way. Indian petroglyphs dating back about one thousand years are found in the general area just north of the Great Stone Face. These markings are now highlighted by a new sign.

To reach this natural wonder, travel to Delta and then go southwest on US 6/50 about five miles and turn south on State Route 257. Then travel about six miles south on SR 257 to a signed turnoff to the west (right). Go west on the gravel road and travel for almost six miles to the north edge of the black lava beds. The gravel road—passable by cars in dry weather, though there are washboard ruts in the road in places and three cattleguards to cross—loops around the west side of the hill and ends at a small parking area. There is no admission fee.

The petroglyphs are located just a few hundred yards before the parking lot and feature their own sign. These inscriptions were jokingly called the first edition of the *Deseret News*, Utah's first newspaper, in the 1920s and 1930s by Millard County newspapers.

Hike south up the hillside, looking for the dominant rock. Those who can't or don't want to hike can still see the Great Stone Face from a distance, best viewed with binoculars.

24

MONTE CRISTO

Utah's Mountain of Christ

U tah has its own "Mountain of Christ," though it is often overlooked—and to this day no one is certain who named it or why.

Monte Cristo means "Mountain of Christ" in Spanish. How that came to be applied to a landscape in northern Utah, far from Spanish and Mexican settlements in New Mexico and California and trade routes through southern Utah, is part of the mystery.

Many decades before a viable seasonal highway (Utah State Road 39) traversed its heights, the Monte Cristo Mountains, about forty miles northwest of Ogden, produced mystery and fascination. Miners had passed by in the 1890s, headed northwest when the nearby La Plata mines of Utah's Cache County were in their brief heyday.

"A grand trip to 'Old Monte,' Near but unknown solitude and grandeur in the Monte Christo [sic] Mountains" was an August 26, 1908 newspaper headline in the *Logan Republican*. "It is distinctly a region of scenery and scenery on a scale of grandeur obtainable in very few places," the story trumpeted, dubbing it Utah's "Garden of the Gods."

"You may drive all day and meet no one, see no signs of habitation, unless it be a lone sheepherder's tent," the story said, observing that sheepmen call the area "Old Monte" and that its greatest charm is solitude and being cut off from the world of humanity.

The *Ogden Standard-Examiner* of August 11, 1910, also reported on the allure of Monte Cristo. It stated that a party of Ogdenites was going to travel there to ascertain the height of the tallest peak, Monte Cristo. Rumors had

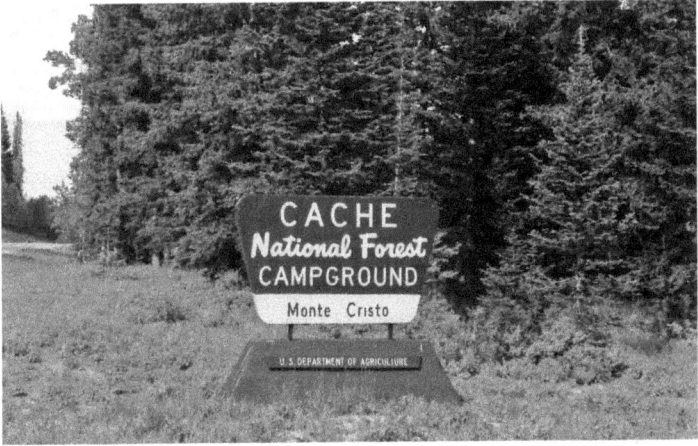

The Monte Cristo area, thirty miles northeast of Huntsville, features a same-named campground, though it is usually snow packed until July. *Lynn Arave photo.*

for several decades, since the La Plata mining boom, suggested the summit to be between eleven and thirteen thousand feet above sea level.

The Monte Cristo mountains are where four Utah counties—Weber, Rich, Cache and Morgan—intersect and where the nearest towns are Huntsville or Woodruff, both about twenty-two bird-flying miles in any straight direction.

The *Salt Lake Tribune* of August 18, 1910, reported on the group's findings: "The height of the mountain, which many in the party had been led to believe was inaccessible and one of the highest in the state, was found to be 8,950 feet above sea level." Modern measurements have upped that elevation to 9,148 feet.

"Monte Cristo, that mysterious peak on the great ridge running between Weber and Rich counties, is a part of the watershed of Camp Kiesel," O.H. Bybee wrote in the July 2, 1926 *Ogden Standard-Examiner*. Bybee had recently hiked to Monte Cristo Peak from Camp Kiesel, elevation 6,100 feet. He said he had traveled through some of the finest aspen stands he had ever seen and that from the Monte Summit he could see the High Uintas to the east and the Wasatch peaks Mount Ogden and Ben Lomond.

On the way down, he ran across the "fresh trail of a bear not more than 15 minutes before" his own passage. He proclaimed that he was glad he was heading south and not the way that bruin was going.

Who gave the mountains and tallest peak their religious name, Monte Cristo, is apparently a mystery for the ages. According to the book *Utah Place Names*, by John W. Van Cott, there are three different possible origins: First, miners returning from California through the range might have felt the landscape resembled the Monte Cristo Mountains of California. Second, the name could have been bestowed by early French Canadian trappers. And third, it is said that an early road builder working in the area carried a copy of the Alexandre Dumas adventure novel *The Count of Monte Cristo*, which he read to his coworkers at night around the campfire.

However, since the 1908 *Logan Republican* story spotlighted the area's remoteness—and no road was mentioned, but the place-name "Monte" was already familiar—that lends credence to only the first two origin stories.

The first road to Monte Cristo Peak area was built from 1927 to 1928. The fact that the peak was named before Highway 39 was constructed indicates that road builders did not name the peak. It was likely named three decades earlier, during the era of the La Plata mining boom.

25

DEVIL'S GATE

Pioneer Bugaboo

Salt Lake City might not have become Utah's first city—and a regional crossroads—if the "devil" hadn't gotten in the way of Mormon pioneers and other trailblazers in the 1840s.

In a June 13, 1914 article, the *Ogden Standard-Examiner* lamented the community's lost destiny under a headline that read: "Ogden Might Have Been the One Big City in the State of Utah." As it turned out, Weber Canyon's Devil's Gate deterred the Mormon pioneers from the more direct lower Weber Canyon through the Wasatch Mountains. Instead, they detoured southwest and into the Salt Lake Valley.

Here's a "what if?" scenario: It is July 21, 1847, and Orson Pratt and Erastus Snow, advance scouts for the first party of pioneer settlers, emerge from the mountains into the valley of the Great Salt Lake. A day later, on July 22, most of the rest of the wagon caravan—143 men, 3 women and 2 children, members of the Church of Jesus Christ of Latter-day Saints—roll into the valley.

Then, on July 24, the wagon of their leader, Brigham Young, delayed by illness, leaves Weber Canyon and enters the valley—at today's South Weber and Uintah, towns along the Weber River.

"This is the right place," Young proclaims. "Drive on."

But that is NOT how it happened.

The pioneer party instead turned south at today's Henefer toward East Canyon, Big Mountain, Little Dell and Little Mountain—a challenging route followed a year earlier by the mishap- and tragedy-plagued Donner

Devil's Gate is now an isolated alcove with a dirt road circling it and the railroad traversing it. Interstate highway construction blasted away thousands of tons of rock to bypass it. *Lynn Arave photo.*

Party in 1846—and arrived in their "promised valley" via Emigration Canyon instead.

If fiendishly cramped and winding Devil's Gate, near the mouth of Weber Canyon, had not been so formidable a gorge for wagons, Ogden or some other place farther north might have become key and centerpiece to the settlement of Utah.

Weber Canyon, named for trapper and trader John Henry Weber, was a section of what was then being called the "Hastings Cutoff," a "shortcut" to California off the earlier Oregon Trail promoted by Lansford Hastings. An 1846 map made by T.H. Jefferson identified the Devil's Gate area as "Granite Canyon."

But at the bottom of Devil's Gate, the wild Weber River churned over rocks in a deep, narrow crevice, with no obvious way to avoid the treacherous cascade. The canyon there was only wide enough to handle the river, perhaps horses, and not much else—let alone wagons.

Heinrich Lienhard, a frontiersman in Jefferson's party, described his wagon passage through Devil's Gate as the wildest part of his journey across the wilderness of the West. In his diary account for August 6, 1846, he recorded:

Utah Heaven and Hell

The Weber River had broken down the steep, high Wasatch Mountains; it was a deep cleft through which the waters foamed and roared over the rocks.

We ventured upon this furious passage, up to this point decidedly the wildest we had encountered, if not the most dangerous. We devoted the entire forenoon and until fully one o'clock in the afternoon to the task of getting our four wagons though....

In going back for each wagon we had to be very careful lest we lose our footing on the slippery rocks under the water and ourselves be swept down the rapid, foaming torrent.

That same year, the Allen and Avery group recorded its passage through the "Granite Canyon" area, and for them, it required grueling teamwork and sturdy rope to hoist wagons and oxen through the narrow passage.

Apparently, the name "Granite Canyon" on that early map wasn't scary enough for passing emigrants. Instead, the "devil" seemed to deserve credit, or blame, for the obnoxious gorge preventing safe wagon passage westward.

Legendary Mormon explorer, and later lawman, Porter Rockwell led advance scouts in a reconnaissance of lower Weber Canyon during the 1847 pioneer trek. They found the gorge worse than Hastings, who had diverted the Donner Party from the obstacle, and others had described it.

The 1914 *Standard* article observed that wagons had to be taken piecemeal through Devil's Gate in pioneer times, their loads carried separately down-canyon on pack horses along a nearby Indian path. The article also speculated that if the Donner Party had traveled down Weber Canyon instead in early September 1846, perhaps the Mormon pioneers would have done so, too, in July 1847. However, the scouts' recommendation to Brigham Young was to go through Emigration Canyon instead.

It is said that Brigham Young had a divine vision of the area of the Salt Lake Valley, in which his people were to settle. That is often given as a reason why the pioneer party still might have turned south and traveled some thirty miles over daunting passes and through additional canyons to the site of today's Salt Lake City, via Emigration Canyon.

If not for the road not taken, today's South Weber or Layton—or Ogden—or some other location might have become today's Salt Lake City. Mountain man and fur trader Miles Goodyear had already established and was living at Fort Buenaventura, laying claim to everything between Weber and Ogden canyons along the face of the Wasatch Mountains. The fort is considered the first permanent non-Indian settlement in the Great Basin. Goodyear subsequently sold his interests to the Mormons, and the city that eventually did take root there came to be known as Ogden—named for yet another fur trader, Hudson's Bay Company brigade leader Peter Skene Ogden.

Devil's Gate would be partially tamed eight years after the pioneers' arrival, in 1855. At that time, Thomas Jefferson Thurston, Abiah Wadsworth (one of co-author Lynn Arave's ancestors), Ira Spaulding, Charles Peterson, Roswell Stevens and other prospective settlers built a road up Weber Canyon from South Weber and by Devil's Gate into the promising Morgan Valley. Thurston had accidentally come upon the Morgan Valley while scrambling over the mountain ridge above his Centerville home. The favorable-looking valley below seemed similar to his former home in Ohio.

The roadbuilders had only primitive tools at their disposal, and sometimes huge rocks would simply be pushed off from the walls above the gorge so a road could be made on top of such fill material. That first road was completed by 1856.

Thurston Peak, the highest point in both Davis and Morgan Counties, atop the Wasatch ridge line, was later named for Thomas Jefferson Thurston.

As it turned out, Devil's Gate did prove to have a beneficial, "angelic" side. In 1868–69, the route of the Transcontinental Railroad came right through Weber Canyon. Conquering the obstructive gorge gave Mormon Utahns two years of employment by the Union Pacific Railroad, in 1868 and 1869, in Weber Canyon and areas east.

Years later, Devil's Gate was opened to one-lane passage with the construction of Horseshoe Bend, a loop in the road around Devil's Gate. Families entering from either side of Devil's Gate by horse and buggy would send one person ahead on foot to stop traffic on the narrow path while they passed through.

The route through Weber Canyon bedeviled travelers for generations. Devil's Gate definitely proved to be more devilish a landmark than Devil's Slide, a peculiar cleft twenty-three miles to the east. A Devil's Chair rock formation, just east of Devil's Gate, also had a measure of fame at the time.

And an 1887 article in the *Ogden Standard-Examiner* referred to the west end of Weber Canyon as the "Devil's Road," due to the rough and rocky conditions of Devil's Gate. Weber County and Morgan County, connected by the route, even disputed over which should maintain the bridge at Devil's Gate.

The devilment continued over the decades.

The *Salt Lake Herald* reported "a snow slide and wreck at Devil's Gate" in a January 10, 1892 headline and story. An eighty-foot-deep, one-hundred-foot-wide slide plummeted into the canyon at Devil's Gate, covering and damaging the railroad tracks. A freight train going through was unable to stop in time and crashed into the debris. An engineer was killed, and six railcars smashed.

A December 21, 1893 story in the *Davis County Clipper* described Devil's Gate and its Horseshoe Bend as a dangerous "man trap." The newspaper described the passage as perilous, not only because of the "old banging bridge" that had to be crossed, and which hung precariously by the side of the mountain, but also due to the threat of one hundred tons of rock hanging overhead, ready to cut loose and fall at any time. Even then, Devil's Gate lurked in the realm of "Satanic majesty," the story's writer opined— and anyone who safely crossed through the place would thank God on the other side for safely having done so.

By the early automobile age, the road through Devil's Gate had been widened to two lanes. It continued, however, to earned new nicknames. One such was Scrambled-Egg Curve because of the frequent accidents involving trucks transporting along the winding route, along with other cargo spills: livestock, vegetables and even oil. The "devil" simply could not be conquered.

After the wet winter of 1952, flood waters cut off travel through Devil's Gate for several weeks. Commuters from Morgan County trying to drive west had to park vehicles on the east side of the narrows and walk around Devil's Gate to get rides to work from the other side.

Construction of the interstate highway system eventually transformed Devil's Gate. Dynamite, heavy equipment and shifts of workers were brought in during the early 1960s to clear a path around and above the gorge for the construction of two 583-foot-long concrete bridges, key components in completing Interstate 80 North—now I-84.

The bugaboo that had been Devil's Gate and Scrambled Egg Curve was finally vanquished. The project cost $2.5 million at the time—almost $22 million in 2020 dollars—to build the three-mile freeway section.

Today it is not easy to spot Devil's Gate in lower Weber Canyon. Motorists zoom through the area at up to sixty-five miles per hour, hardly slowing down for what might have been the only truly insurmountable barrier the Mormon pioneers faced during their historic trek.

With more and faster traffic at the location than ever, there doesn't even seem to be a safe place to visit the site. The interstate highway makes a slight bend at Devil's Gate now, just west of the Weber-Morgan county line.

The canyon's ancient carver, the Weber River, still makes a loop northward at rockbound Devil's Gate. Remnants of the old Horseshoe Bend roadway are visible, far below. A train trestle, a reminder of the Transcontinental Railroad and succeeding bridges that crossed the river here, is nearby.

Devil's Gate has become a twisty, isolated alcove, a Weber River chasm probably frequented by only an occasional fisherman.

26

DEVIL'S SLIDE

Wicked Chute

U nlike Devil's Gate, which has been heavily dynamited and bypassed by today's interstate, Devil's Slide farther east in Weber Canyon looks much as it did in pioneer times and during passenger travel on the Transcontinental Railroad and is readily visible along the freeway.

Devil's Slide is an eye-catching limestone chute on the south side of I-84 and the Weber River in Weber Canyon, near Croydon and about eight miles east of Morgan.

The feature is composed of two parallel upturned slabs of sedimentary rock formed at the bottom of a shallow sea some 170 to 180 million years ago. In the mountain-building eons since then, the layers have been upturned and eroded, forming the chute with sides about twenty feet apart, some forty feet high and several hundred feet long, the Utah Geological Survey explains. A softer middle layer, more susceptible to erosion, has weathered away more, creating the devilish channel.

The first pioneers through the area in the 1840s (and their maps) referred to the Croydon area of upper Weber Canyon as "Gutter Defile," in honor of what would eventually become famous as Devil's Slide.

Who named the rock formation Devil's Slide?

James John Walker (1830–1896), an early resident of Croydon and a railroad worker, might be the first person to have called it Devil's Slide. A Walker family history says that Walker was a contractor on the Transcontinental Railroad, helping install the first tracks through upper Weber Canyon. Probably around 1868, he was asked (being a local resident)

Weber Canyon's Devil's Slide has been a landmark since pioneer emigrants headed for California passed by. *Ray Boren photo.*

by a railroad crew what to call the unusual rocky chute. His reply was "Devil's Slide," and the name stuck. The first known mention of that name in a newspaper was in 1875.

"Looking like a large playground slide fit only for the Devil, this site is a tilted remnant of sediments deposited in a sea that occupied Utah's distant geologic past," Carl Ege of the Utah Geological Survey explains on geology. utah.gov.

By 1904, the limestone found in abundance in the area of Devil's Slide drew the attention of cement makers. Soon, a cement worker's town sprang up there. Workers initially called the new community Portland, in honor of the Union Portland Cement Co. However, railroad people objected to that name and insisted on calling it Devil's Slide instead. They won out, and by 1907, the local post office was also called Devils Slide—without an apostrophe.

The cement company's packaging for Red Devil Cement sported the startling image of a red-tinted devil sliding down a slope on his pitchfork. The company's baseball team was also called the Red Devils.

The little town reached its heyday in the late 1920s, before the Great Depression, when it boasted 529 residents. By the 1940s, its school had

The middle interior of Devil's Slide, looking down toward the Weber River. *Lynn Arave photo.*

Venice Carson Flygare of Ogden poses in front of Devil's Slide in 1947, when the highway ran right next to it in the pre-freeway era. *Flygare-Arave family photo.*

closed, and by the 1980s, only a few families still resided there. Soon after, the cement company closed the town, and today, a quarry and rubble mostly cover what remains of the ghost town.

More than a century ago, on September 16, 1910, the *Salt Lake Tribune* headlined a story, "Devil's Slide jinks success; El Kalah Temple Mystic Shrine holds unique ceremonial at that spot; Novices slide incline into fathomless pool." Several hundred Shriners took a special train to the slide and even set up tents in the area. The Shriners somehow found a way to slide down Devil's Slide.

Ogden's *Standard* reported on the Shriners' festive antics the next year. "Mystic Shriners at Devil's Slide," read the headline over a story published on August 22, 1911. The Shriners held special ceremonies and initiations around the formation, the story says. Included was a hike to the top of the formation, followed by an optional daring slide down toward the Weber River

Did this really happen? Perhaps. But the natural chute ends many feet away from the river, which is why a special pool of water was apparently set up at the bottom by the Shriners.

Ogden began promoting Devil's Slide as a tourist attraction with directional highway signs in the mid-1920s.

Today, posted turnouts alert motorists to viewpoints off both directions of I-84. However, a 1947 photograph of Devil's Slide, taken in the pre-freeway era, shows the viewing area of the time was much closer to the formation than it is today. Back then, what is now a dirt access road to private land, which is in front of Devil's Slide, might have been the main canyon road before the interstate came along. Now the slide's bottom is choked with brush.

Hauntingly, otherworldly references are common in upper Weber Canyon. Witch Rocks and the small Goblin Slides rock formations are not too far away.

An early *Salt Lake Tribune* story, published on June 28, 1888, told a tale about an out-of-stater fishing the Weber River in this vicinity with an Indian guide. The Native American believed the area to be the devil's territory and even pointed out another nearby rock formation, said to be the "Devil's War Club."

As unusual as northern Utah's Devil's Slide might seem, it is not unique, even by that name. Among others, there is a same-named and similar rock formation on Cinnabar Mountain, above US 89 about five miles north of Gardiner, Montana, and near Yellowstone National Park. That Devil's Slide, though, has a twist—literally: a big curve amid its long course of parallel rock.

27

GOG AND MAGOG

Twin Rugged Peaks

They have to be the two most strangely named mountain peaks in Utah: Gog and Magog. While there's no doubt they were named after biblical references in the Books of Ezekiel and Revelation, exactly why they were so named is a mystery. But a hike on the area's White Pine Trail, which travels between the two peaks and to White Pine Lake, is well worth the effort.

Gog and Magog are definitely rugged, and that could have something to do with them being named after two representations of evil—probably nations or peoples rather than individuals—that, according to some religious scholars, oppose God's plans and Israel. The two summits also tower above all but two peaks in the area north of Tony Grove and Logan Canyon, near the Utah-Idaho border.

Mount Magog, the southernmost peak and the one visible from Tony Grove Lake, is 9,756 feet above sea level. Tony Grove Lake sits at an elevation of 8,050. Gog rises to an altitude of 9,700 feet, and although it is not as jagged and rough-hewn from all viewpoints as Magog, it would be a formidable mountain to climb for most.

The first local newspaper mention of the peaks was in the Salt Lake Herald of August 30, 1887. A Utah artist, H.L. Culmer, had painted a scene of the area. Titled *Lake Magog at Sunset*, the work showcased both summits and the small body of water, now named White Pine Lake, in between.

Some years later, in 1896, a controversy arose over that lake being called Lake Magog. The *Journal* newspaper of Logan, Utah, published an opinion

Mount Gog, above Tony Grove and Logan Canyon, is a biblically named feature.
Lynn Arave photo.

piece that lakes should have feminine titles, while peaks should espouse the masculine names.

According to Chip Sibbernsen, former recreation manager for the Logan Ranger District, the hike from Tony Grove to White Pine Lake and the Gog/ Magog Peaks lures hikers to use the popular White Pine Trail, so weekends and holidays are usually crowded. He suggests midweek use for solitude on the pleasant hike.

Because the trail generally climbs so gradually, except along the final switchbacks to White Pine Lake, mountain bikes also frequently use the trail, as do riders and horses. The trek is also suitable for young children, according to a hiking guide for kids.

The trail is usable after spring snowmelt, which means sometime in June most years. It remains traversable until late September or early October, depending on the weather.

The trail begins at the north end of Tony Grove Lake and follows the same trail as the Mount Naomi path for the first four hundred yards. Then they separate. The White Pine Trail travels though pretty meadows and is generally wide and well-marked. However, a spilt in the trail at the three-quarters of a mile mark is confusing. Here, hikers should stay to the right and go east around the base of a hill instead of turning west.

The route crosses several streams and at three miles out reaches an overlook—a good place for taking photographs of Gog and Magog, with

Magog on the left. Switchbacks then descend one mile to the lake at the west end of the valley.

White Pine Valley is well forested but can be swampy, with mosquitoes. The lake itself is a smaller version of Tony Grove's lake—another cirque lake—but a quieter one. Campsites and a restroom are near the lake. A China Wall–like rock formation separates the Gog and Magog peaks above White Pine Lake.

Many trails crisscross the Tony Grove area. There's a 3.2-mile trail to Mount Naomi—the area's tallest peak at 9,980 feet—another to Doubletop Mountain (9,872 feet), a northeast path to US 89 and others that lead to and from the Cache Valley.

The mountains and destinations east of the Cache Valley have received a fair share of newspaper coverage, dating to the nineteenth century.

"Camp at Tony Grove" was an August 15, 1897 report in the *Logan Journal*. This might be the first recorded account of recreational camping in the area, just north of Logan Canyon, Utah. "There is a merry crowd of campers at Tony Grove in Logan Canyon," the newspaper read. At least 125 people were camped there then, "enjoying the exquisite scenery, the fresh bracing air, the cool days and nights, refreshing sleep, fishing and all the pleasures of an unceremonious canyon existence." During the evening, the campers gathered for a large bonfire party, with music, singing and games by moonlight. Many planned to spend another week or two.

Indeed, according to the book *Utah Place Names* by John W. Van Cott, the Tony Grove name originated from the loggers and cattlemen of the 1880s who would observe all of the well-to-do "tony" people who could afford to camp and stay in the area for long stretches in the summer. The name eventually transitioned from the people to the place.

The *Ogden Standard-Examiner* on June 29, 1924, reported the largest excursion ever to visit Logan Canyon and the lake, with up to six hundred students and faculty of the Utah Agricultural College converging at Tony Grove. The school had sponsored such a day to Tony Grove since at least 1920.

The group spent the day hiking and playing games. They even explored a remote cave on the mountainside, descending by rope to its opening. It was said to be located above better-known Logan Cave. They hiked to area landmarks like White Pine Lake, Gog and Magog and Mount Naomi.

Opposite: Mount Magog is a rugged pinnacle above White Pine Lake in an area north of Logan Canyon. *Lynn Arave photo.*

PART V

FORGOTTEN PLACES

28

FREMONT ISLAND

Grave Robber to Phantom Coyote

Among the most legendary of pre-Mormon pioneer religious artifacts in Utah—yet one difficult to access and see—is a small cross that famed Western guide Kit Carson created one day on lonely Fremont Island in the Great Salt Lake. Only about six inches long, the curious landmark dates to September 9, 1843, when Carson carved it on solid rock while his commander and colleague, U.S. Army explorer and mapmaker John C. Frémont, surveyed the area.

Frémont had dubbed the isle "Disappointment Island" for its barren nature and lack of game and water. Carson was apparently so bored that he took the time to chisel the cross. Reports and writings about Fremont's explorations prove that Carson is the one who made the cross.

Carson's biography, for instance, states that he had converted to Catholicism, after being Protestant, some years before his visit to Fremont Island, so his cross has been interpreted as a personal Catholic symbol or relic predating the arrival of Mormonism, which would become the area's dominant religion less than five years later.

The cross hasn't always been definitively credited to Carson, however. For example, "New Speculation Arises About Island Cross" was the headline for a story in the November 2, 1943 edition of the *Ogden Standard-Examiner.* The story questioned the cross's origin, hypothesizing that a bored sheepherder in the 1850s had probably created it.

Soon thereafter, however, it was universally accepted that Carson was indeed the author of the cross.

Fremont Island as it appears from the waterless and drying bed of Great Salt Lake. *Lynn Arave photo.*

On that late summer day in 1843, Fremont, Carson and two other men had followed the Weber River and used an "India rubber" boat to float and paddle to the island directly west of present-day Hooper, Utah. They hoped it would be a little paradise in the desert. However, their reconnaissance left them disappointed. The real excitement came shortly after they left the island. Threatened by an incoming thunderstorm, the party frantically rowed for their lives to get off the wind-whipped Great Salt Lake.

The cross is found at the north end of Fremont Island on what is known as Castle Rock, the isle's high point, rising some eight hundred feet above the average elevation of the Great Salt Lake. Large black rocks dominate this portion of the island, and one of the monoliths hosts the cross, a small marking by comparison. Other than a few metal lightning rods in the area, a deterrent to lightning-caused fires, this section of Fremont Island has likely changed little in the 175-plus years since the cross was carved there.

Some four and a half years after Frémont and Carson and their party were the first known men of European descent to visit the island, Mormon

The famed Kit Carson Cross on the north end of Fremont Island. This Catholic relic predates arrival of Mormon pioneers in the area. *Lynn Arave photo.*

pioneers set foot on the isle on April 22, 1848. They named it Castle Island for the throne-like prominence on its north end—today's Castle Rock.

These early explorers, of course, were not Fremont Island's first visitors. Many Native America relics, including arrowheads, tools and bowls, have been found, indicating earlier, prehistoric habitation.

Howard Stansbury, a U.S. government surveyor, came to Fremont Island in the summer of 1850, during his two-year survey of the Great Salt Lake. He officially named it after Frémont. However, in 1859 and for some years afterward, the island was also known as Miller's Island, when Dan Miller and Henry W. Jacob of Farmington had 153 sheep grazing there.

As punishment, Brigham Young exiled a notorious Salt Lake City grave robber, Jean Baptiste, to Fremont Island in the spring of 1862. Baptiste subsequently vanished and was never seen again.

A few decades later, Salt Lake probate judge Uriah James (U.J.) Wenner and his young family, including children, lived on otherwise uninhabited Fremont Island, from 1886 to 1891, homesteading and raising sheep. Wenner had tuberculosis, and it was hoped that the climate and open air

The stone grave marker of U.J. Wenner and Kate Wenner Noble on Fremont Island. Their family were early settlers on the Great Salt Lake isle. *Lynn Arave photo.*

of the inland sea would temper his illness. However, he died on Fremont in September 1891 and is buried there. The ashes of Kate, his wife, were also buried there after her death in 1941.

From a distance and Great Salt Lake shorelines, Fremont is a long, thin-looking island with a flat plateau on its north end. From many perspectives, it almost seems to be an extension of nearby Promontory Point and the Promontory Mountains to the north. A segment of the island juts out to the west, long enough to land an airplane on it, though this feature is not visible from along the Wasatch Front.

The horses and sheep of those who settled on or used Fremont weren't the only animals to inhabit the island. A tale is told about a "phantom coyote" that eluded determined hunters for more than two weeks in the mid-1940s. The coyote, believed to have hitchhiked to the island on a rare chunk of iceberg in the Great Salt Lake, had killed some fifteen of the eight hundred sheep grazing there. An army of dogs and twenty armed men was dispatched to hunt down the criminal canine.

"Phantom of Isle Still Eludes Dogs" and "Phantom Coyote Has Hunters Marooned in Lake" were two resulting headlines in the *Ogden Standard-Examiner*, from March 26 and March 29, 1944, respectively. High winds not only caused the dogs to lose scent of the coyote but also prevented the hunters from leaving Fremont.

"Hunters again foiled in Phantom Coyote chase; New expedition scheduled," the *Standard-Examiner* reported on March 31, 1944. Hunters joked about needing a silver bullet to stop the animal, as numerous regular bullets had proved ineffective.

Finally, on the fifteenth day of the hunt, "Island Coyote Killed in Lake Waters" was the headline on April 4 in the *Salt Lake Tribune*. A shot had wounded the coyote, so it jumped into the lake and tried to swim away. A motorboat caught up to the animal, which was hauled aboard and killed.

Four other coyotes had been speedily dispatched on Fremont Island in 1942, after they had killed numerous sheep, but none were as elusive as the phantom.

29

MALAN HEIGHTS

Copacabana of the West

One of Utah's most lauded resorts in the late nineteenth century wasn't along the shores of the Great Salt Lake but rather in the Wasatch Mountains, east of Ogden. Malan's Heights was a recreational paradise, by all reports. Some hailed it as the "Copacabana of the West."

"Malan's Heights. B. Malan has now completed a road to Waterfall Canyon and is prepared to accommodate any number of pleasure seekers," the *Standard-Examiner* of August 20, 1895, announced. "It is the best resort in Weber County. Rates for round trip $1 from end of Twenty-fifth street car line. Carriages leaving at 8 a.m."

A narrow wagon road, in the making since 1893, went up Taylor Canyon to what would be known as Malan's Peak and Malan's Basin. Yet in 1895, Waterfall Canyon was likely the only place in that area most Ogdenites knew, outside of the Malan family.

Bartholomew Malan had secured rights to eight hundred acres of mountain land in 1891 and constructed the road with the help of his sons. Some passengers had been transported along the road a year earlier, in 1894, but Malan didn't advertise his resort until the next year.

There would soon be a two-story hotel, a sawmill, seven cabins and a clubhouse, all built, owned and operated by the Malan family on about ten acres. "2,000 feet above the city of Ogden and 6,500 feet above sea level up amongst the pines and loveliest of mountain breezes, so cool and refreshing, having just partaken of a good wholesome dinner, I am now sitting in one

Malan's Basin as it appears today, in the shadow of Mount Ogden. In the 1890s, a lofty mountain resort flourished here. *Lynn Arave photo.*

of the two-seated conveyances that brought four of us up a rocky serpentine road 2,000 feet and seven miles from the city," Mrs. L.L. Rogers reported in her "Trip to Malan Heights" in the August 29, 1895 *Standard-Examiner*.

Visitors could get lodging and meals for six dollars a week, while individual meals cost from thirty-five to fifty cents. Fried chicken was the hotel specialty. As many as one hundred patrons at a time visited the new resort, though only a dozen at a time could eat in the small hotel dining room.

There's little doubt that hikers and runners would have no path to access the basin today, or at least would have needed a different route, if the Malan family hadn't pioneered their wagon road.

"You must pay Ten cents toll" was an August 9, 1896 *Standard* headline. Mr. Malan was forced to levy such a toll to each pedestrian using his road because of vandalism. Some people purposely pulled rocks down onto the road or hurled stones, endangering those below. A man was hired to collect the toll and perform upkeep on the road.

A *Standard-Examiner* report on June 5, 1899, stated, "The visitors exclaim they never saw anything like the mountain scenery of the Wasatch Range near Ogden." Baseball, horseshoes, croquet and hiking up to Observatory Peak (later named Mount Ogden) were among the activities there.

Following a ten-year run, the resort closed for good after Malan's sons grew up and sought other employment. The Malans had moved to 2720 Taylor Avenue in Ogden, and Bartholomew Malan died in 1913.

Although the resort in Malan's Basin closed at the end of the 1904 summer season, plans were soon underway to improve and open it again. "New Resort Planned. Electric Line to Malan Heights, overlooking Ogden" was a May 31, 1905 headline in the *Ogden Standard-Examiner*. David Mattson, the Weber County clerk, had secured a one-year option on the land and then an option to purchase it. Mattson wanted to improve the wagon road to the resort and eventually put a rail line in.

"Mr. Mattson is very enthusiastic over the proposition and states it is his intention to establish a hotel, dance halls, etc., on the heights and no pains will be spared to make the place attractive," the *Standard* reported. Those plans fell through, though.

By February 1907, additional plans were underway. Thomas Slight, a local artist, was painting a large picture of Malan's Heights. It was to be given to engineers to design a cog railroad to Malan's Basin and even a dam for a lake in the basin.

"Cable to the clouds. Phil O'Mara and Associates to build to Observatory Peak," read a March 12, 1907 *Standard* headline. The proposal called for the resort site to be enlarged and renamed "Haven."

Again, the dreams were for naught: "Will Be No Resort at Malan Heights," the Ogden newspaper announced shortly thereafter, on June 30, 1907, citing "too many obstacles in the way to procuring clear titles to the property."

The *Salt Lake Tribune* subsequently informed readers that most of what was left of the resort burned down on November 8, 1910, in a forest fire caused by careless hunters. A *Standard-Examiner* report on December 20, 1910, also noted that almost all of the resort buildings had been burned by campers in the previous two years.

In succeeding years, vandalism and theft plagued the old resort property. Trespassing herds of sheep destroyed growing trees. Boys and men cut down trees to sell at Christmastime. A December 20, 1910 *Standard* story indicated that up to one hundred evergreen trees had been stolen from the private land, and trees valued at about $1,000 had been burned.

"Electric sign on the Heights" signaled the next failed chapter in the site's history, as described in the July 18, 1912 *Standard*. Ogdenite Gus Wright wanted the Ogden Publicity Bureau to put a glitzy "Ogden" sign—to be illuminated by electric light bulbs—on Malan's Point (today's Malan's Peak) to attract the attention of train travelers. That never happened.

"Campers Endangered by a Gang at Malan's" was a July 20, 1915 *Standard* headline. Some fifty picnickers in Malan's Basin were terrorized by an unknown group of men who fired guns in all directions and eventually forced everyone else off the mountain.

"Notice to the public. We have leased Malan Heights for grazing purposes. Do not trespass. Hansen Livestock & Feeding Company," warned a June 4, 1918 advertisement in the *Standard*.

A May 22, 1923 *Standard* report mentioned a plan by William R. Miller to establish another pleasure resort in Malan's grove, complete with a ten-mile automobile road and railroad access. Miller had a lease on 1,100 acres, with an option to buy from G.H. Malan. The July 4, 1923 *Standard* reported that Miller had a temporary store, food and refreshments for hikers available in Malan's Basin—for that summer only. Groups of Boy Scouts and Girl Scouts also camped there that summer, but no permanent resort was realized.

A steam boiler is the largest relic that still remains in Malan's Basin, where a hotel and cabins prospered at the end of the nineteenth century. *Lynn Arave photo.*

On September 13, 1925, the Young People's Society of Ogden's First Methodist/Episcopal Church held Sunday services at Malan's Heights.

Then, another big fire on September 5, 1927, destroyed anything left in Malan's Basin.

More recently, in 2005–6 businessman Chris Peterson purchased 1,140 acres in and around Malan's Basin, hoping to develop a year-round resort featuring skiing and accessibility by lift or gondola. This modern-day proposal hasn't worked out either. And sadly, vandalism—tree carving, equipment destruction, littering—continues to plague the historic mountain property.

30

WEBER POWER PLANT

Marvel of Its Time

R acing down Weber Canyon today, it might be difficult to notice, but just east of the mouth of Weber Canyon and two miles west of Devil's Gate is an antique-looking hydroelectric power plant squeezed between Interstate 84's four lanes of traffic. The power plant dates to 1910 and harnesses the currents of the Weber River.

Its beginnings are a tale of financial woes and an often-uncooperative Mother Nature, but the plant's survival for over a century is worth pondering.

Electricity to power cities, industries, businesses and homes took off phenomenally in the late nineteenth century. Small hydroelectric projects popped up in almost every canyon on both sides of the Wasatch Mountains, tapping into rivers and even small streams in the 1890s and after the turn of the twentieth century. It is remarkable how many of these small, often brick edifices remain—marvels of their time and still generating power to this day.

According to the *Deseret Evening News* of April 26, 1900, the Weber Canyon power plant was proposed that spring. Charles K. Bannister, a civil engineer who designed an electric power plant for Ogden Canyon, was also designing this one. It would not interfere with irrigation supplies and would help provide power from Ogden to Salt Lake to Park City.

The *Salt Lake Herald Republican* newspaper of April 26 that year reported that a 360-foot-long tunnel that used a pipe six feet in a diameter would be used to send water to the turbines. The story said Ogden Canyon's power plant was already nearing capacity, so another plant in Weber Canyon was desperately needed.

The power plant intake from the Weber River for the new electrical generating facility in Weber Canyon, about 1909. The plant has been operational since 1910. *Utah State Historical Society.*

The *Ogden Daily Standard* of April 27, 1900, boasted that the new power plant "will make Ogden the greatest electrical power center in the west."

Unfortunately, financial problems hindered the project's undertaking. In fact, for years some northern Utah newspapers referred to the project as a "Big Power Scheme," since little progress was made. The *Ogden Daily Standard* of February 3, 1903, said the plant would be operational by the fall. It wasn't. The *Ogden Daily Standard* of June 7, 1904, predicted work would begin that year. It didn't. The *Salt Lake Herald* of December 7, 1905, reported that Frank Y. Taylor of Utah National Bank had finally applied with the State of Utah for water diversion rights.

The *Deseret News* of May 2, 1906, indicated that $6,000 had been spent on the project so far but urged patience since the project would require considerable time. By the end of 1907, $25,000 had been spent on the power plant project, according to the *Salt Lake Herald Republican* of December 30. At that point, the effort was on winter hiatus.

In the summer of 1908, the project finally jumped into high gear. The *Davis Clipper* newspaper of August 28 said that work tents were "scattered all over on both sides of the [Weber] River." The *Salt Lake Tribune* of November 22, 1908, reported that two hundred men and fifty horse teams were working on the power project, with total costs expected to soar to $400,000 (about $10.6 million in 2020).

Washouts by the flooding river, landslides and even snow slides hindered the project in its final two years, according to the *Salt Lake Telegram* of March 29, 1909.

Ground was finally broken on the actual power plant building in the fall of 1909, according to the *Ogden Daily Standard* of October 1, 1909. The *Salt Lake Tribune* of February 4, 1910, referred to it as a "mammoth power station" by that era's standards, capable of generating up to five thousand horsepower—double the original estimate.

In the summer of 1910, a decade after its shaky, uncertain beginnings, the Weber Canyon hydroelectric plant finally became a reality. According to the July 26, 1910 *Salt Lake Tribune*, the Utah Light and Railway Co. constructed the original facility, which was lauded as the "largest of its kind in the world." A small retention dam—110 feet long and 14 feet wide—had been constructed a half-mile east to provide the water for the plant's aqueduct.

The Weber plant has been improved and modernized over the decades. Now referred to as the Devil's Gate–Weber Hydropower Plant, it is operated by Rocky Mountain Power.

31

LAKE PARK

Prequel to Lagoon

L agoon, one of the nation's oldest amusement parks and the largest between the Midwest and the California coast, does not reside in its original location, nor does it sport its original name.

Lake Park, Lagoon's forerunner, began on the shores of the Great Salt Lake, about three miles southwest of today's theme park in Farmington, Utah, beyond the western end of present-day Clark Lane. Lake Park was promoted as one of the "most attractive watering places in the west." It encompassed 215 acres and existed for about nine years there.

Utahns in the late 1800s loved their Great Salt Lake, where they could "float like a cork" in the buoyant salt water, and the original resort capitalized on that popularity.

Railroad magnate and entrepreneur Simon Bamberger—later elected Utah's first-ever Democratic governor in 1917—pushed hard to develop Lake Park in 1886, hoping to attract large crowds from Salt Lake County and to increase traffic on his interurban railroad line.

Bamberger, better known by Utah residents for the Bamberger Railroad than as the father of Lagoon, built an approximate two-mile spur off the main Denver & Rio Grande Western (D&RGW) line to reach Lake Park Resort.

Although wealthy, Bamberger called on the financial support of other investors, including George Goss and a cousin, Jacob E. Bamberger. Those two contributed $74,950 of the $100,000 needed to start Lake Park. Simon Bamberger added $23,000, and two others the remainder, according to the *Salt Lake Herald* of June 25, 1886.

Lake Park Resort, on the shore of Great Salt Lake in Farmington, as it appeared with direct railroad access in the early 1890s. *Utah State Historical Society.*

Approximately fifty-three thousand guests visited the park in 1886. Admission in those days was fifty cents. Swimming, dancing, boating, a merry-go-round pulled by a horse, target shooting, roller skating and bowling were all included for that price. An extra half-dollar provided a full-course meal at the resort's restaurant.

For its premiere season, the resort had fifteen dozen men's and three dozen women's swimming suits available for rent. To help prevent theft, "Lake Park Resort" was written across the fronts of the suits.

There were six trains a day, painted in a Tuscan red, going to Lake Park from Salt Lake City and three a day coming from Ogden. A sailboat racing and a rowing club also had headquarters at Lake Park. The resort also boasted of its open-air dancing pavilion with finely carved archways and lattice and ample electric lighting.

Summer cottages at the site were rented by the day or month. By one account, it even had a small Victorian-style hotel and a string of cabins along the beach.

The main pavilion was 3,600 square feet and flanked on the north by a restaurant, 30-by-60-feet in size, and on the south by a saloon of equal size. On the west was a pier about 150 feet in length. Bathhouses were north and

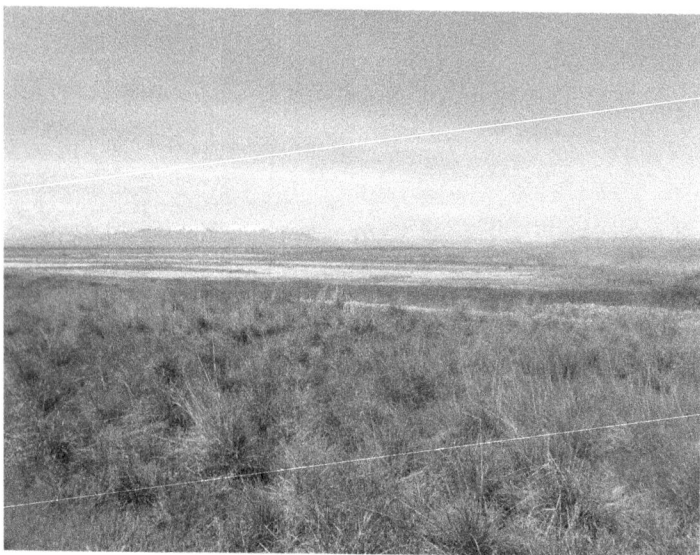

Nothing but a salty plain exists now in the spot where Lake Park, the forerunner resort to today's Lagoon, existed. *Lynn Arave photo.*

south of the pier. The railroad passenger platform was on the east side of the large pavilion. There were also a dozen round picnic houses covered with green ivy and with tables underneath them.

Many Farmington residents would simply walk to Lake Park for an outing. And although it was billed as a bathing resort, boat races and footraces were also popular events at Lake Park. An advertisement in the August 3, 1887 *Deseret Evening News* said the resort also had a shooting gallery, a baseball field, cricket grounds, a racetrack, a gymnasium and its own orchestra. It also offered boat rides to "Church Island," today's Antelope Island in the Great Salt Lake.

However, by 1895, the resort was suffering. The once-high Great Salt Lake was receding, approaching its average surface elevation of 4,200 feet above sea level.

What was once the lakeshore had become a sticky, blue-colored mud that swimmers began to shun. It would have required a walk through muddy and smelly salt flats of a third of a mile or more to reach the lake edge. Then, it would have been another long walk to reach water deep enough to swim.

In the mid-1890s, Bamberger decided to move the resort eastward. For his new resort location, he purchased from Farmington farmers what then were forty acres of swampy farmland, where noisy bullfrogs croaked—though some stories say the site was a natural meadow. Bamberger had the land graded and then excavated, creating a four-foot-deep lake, though, again, some accounts state that there were actually two large ponds. In any event, the two lakes eventually became one large lake, and the larger is the one in use today. As for the evicted frogs, they were sold as delicacies to Montana mining camps.

The *Davis County Clipper* of November 14, 1895, described the future Lagoon site as a "big slough" that would enlarge as a pond to cover six acres and be four feet deep. It said the price for the land was $2,000.

The *Salt Lake Herald* of January 26, 1896, reported that A.M. Lamb of Farmington was working to remove all of the Lake Park buildings, which were to be reconstructed at the new resort location.

The *Davis County Clipper* of February 28, 1896, informed readers that eight to ten teams of horses were at work hauling the Lake Park pavilion from near the dried-up Great Salt Lake to a new freshwater resort. Days of work were expected for this task.

Eventually, not all of the buildings were moved from the old resort site. The *Salt Lake Herald* of August 25, 1897, reported that a frame house of five or six rooms belonging to Simon Bamberger and near the defunct Lake Park resort was destroyed by a fire. It was thought to have been started by careless young men and was valued at several hundred dollars.

The old Lake Park location thrived as a saltworks extraction area for almost thirty years, until similar enterprises in northern Utah put it out of business. The unused railroad tracks to the area were removed in 1925. By the late winter of 1896, an advertisement in the *Davis County Clipper* sought to pasture cattle, horses and sheep at the former resort site.

The park reopened as Lagoon on Sunday, July 12, 1896, a decade after Lake Park's original debut on the shores of the Great Salt Lake. The opening was also two months later than originally planned.

Visiting Lagoon's original Lake Park location today reveals no obvious signs that a resort and railroad line were ever in the area. A horse ranch, pastures and wetlands dominate the former resort site.

The Great Salt Lake—flirting again with record low levels—is presently nowhere to be seen in the vicinity.

32

THIS IS THE PLACE

The Original

Where is the actual spot Brigham Young is said to have declared, as he looked down on what is now the Salt Lake Valley in 1847: "This is the right place, drive on"?

As it turns out, it isn't where the titanic granite-and-bronze This Is the Place Monument, dedicated in the pioneer centennial year of 1947, sits above the north side of Salt Lake City's Sunnyside Avenue, near the mouth of Emigration Canyon.

The true location is more likely near where a somewhat obscure snow-white marker sits several hundred yards to the northeast of the more-renowned monument, up a steep little hill.

Both monuments are on the south side of today's This Is the Place Heritage Park, which gets its name from a modern, abbreviated phrasing of Brigham Young's gratified utterance.

The simple, ten-foot-tall obelisk was installed by the Young Men's Mutual Improvement Association and was dedicated by LDS church president Heber J. Grant on July 25, 1921, before a crowd of about two thousand people. "This Is the Place," lettering says on one side of the obelisk, below a stylized bison, or buffalo, skull. "Brigham Young. July 24, 1847." The date is celebrated in Utah as Pioneer Day.

"When I take people on tours of the park I like to tell them about this marker—because almost no one knows about it," says Ellis Ivory, executive director of This Is the Place Heritage Park and chairman of the park

The original This Is the Place pioneer marker is located northeast of the modern monument, shown here in the background. *Ray Boren photo.*

foundation's board. And even then, he acknowledges, the obelisk was not the first remembrance on this venerated spot.

Notably, a cross was the site's first formal marker, says Tresha Kramer, the park's director of public and customer relations and marketing.

Even in 1921, there was much debate over the location of the actual site of Brigham Young's pronouncement. Still, "this monument was located here as the definitive answer as to where the event occurred," a plaque near the 1921 monument states.

W.W. Riter was nine years old in 1847, when he and his parents followed Brigham Young, leader of the Church of Jesus Christ of Latter-day Saints, to the Salt Lake Valley. As an octogenarian, he helped researchers identify the correct location. "In his early years, Wilford Woodruff had taken him to the spot and stated that this is exactly where Brigham Young had uttered those important words," the 1921 monument marker states.

Young had emerged from the canyon after the rest of the pioneer caravan. He was ailing, possibly sick from tick-borne Rocky Mountain fever, and riding in Wilford Woodruff's carriage.

Efforts to pinpoint the high valley perspective began in earnest early in the twentieth century. A location study was conducted in 1915 by a committee that included LDS leaders George Albert Smith and Brigham H. Roberts, notes James L. Kimball in *The Encyclopedia of Mormonism*.

A basic wooden slab was placed on the spot in July 1915. And then the cross—taller than a man—was erected by Roberts and some Boy Scouts.

When doing research for a souvenir book, *The Story of This Is the Place Heritage Park*, Kramer and her associates succeeded in tracking down, in the University of Utah's Special Collections, a donated photograph of that wood cross, apparently copied from an old newspaper. Scrutiny of the old photograph reveals that "This Is the Place" is incised on the wooden crossbar. "Brigham Young" is spelled out vertically down the main trunk below.

Kramer says that she was elated at the discovery—and pleased that it showed a cross, a symbol to her of cultural diversity, which has been a theme of the site for generations.

The cross was replaced by the 1921 obelisk, which itself fell into disrepair and obscurity because of the much larger and more popular 1947 monument. That grand creation—adorned with statuary and designed by Utah artist Mahonri M. Young, a grandson of the pioneer leader—was dedicated on July 24, 1947, before a large crowd, estimated to be fifty thousand strong. In addition to the pioneers, its many statues and tableaux recognize the Indians, mountain men, explorers and other emigrants who came before them.

As This Is the Place Heritage Park was being developed, the 1921 marker was rediscovered in the 1990s. It was rededicated on July 21, 1997, by President Boyd K. Packer of the Church of Jesus Christ of Latter-day Saints' Quorum of the Twelve. The monument work was funded and directed by the Mills chapter of the Sons of Utah Pioneers in partnership with Zachary Mahoney, grandson of one of the chapter members who made it his Eagle Scout project.

Not every pioneer expressed excitement over the first view of the Great Salt Lake Valley in 1847. One, Mrs. Harriet Young, was less than pleased, according to the book *Utah in Her Western Setting*, by historian Milton R. Hunter. Harriet Young said, "Weak and weary as I am I would rather go a thousand miles farther than remain in such a forsaken place as this."

The Great Salt Lake Valley had not previously been viewed as a "promised land" in which to settle. Few earlier emigrants to the West, excepting perhaps trader Miles Goodyear to the north and a few overwintering trappers, had thought the region worth settling. For many, it was a country that God forgot, Hunter wrote in *Brigham Young the Colonizer*.

Nevertheless, once President Brigham Young had said the valley was "the right place," his fellow pioneers accepted the fact and went to work.

Forgotten Places

There were 147 members in the vanguard July 1847 pioneer company, including three women and two children. None of this first party died en route—all made it safely to the Salt Lake Valley after a 1,031-mile trek.

Erastus Snow recorded an account of his emergence, on July 21, 1847, from the tangled mouth of Emigration Canyon and his first view of the valley, as Hunter recounts in *Utah in Her Western Setting*:

> *The thicket down the narrows, at the mouth of the* [Emigration] *canyon, was so dense that one could not penetrate through it. I crawled for some distance on my hands and knees through the thickets, until I was compelled to return, admonished to by the rattle of a snake, which lay coiled up under my nose, having almost put my hand on him; but as he gave me the friendly warning, I thanked him and retreated.*
>
> *We raised on to a high point south of the narrows, where we got a view of the Great Salt Lake and this valley, and each of us, without saying a word to the other, instinctively, as if by inspiration, raised our hats from our heads, and then, swinging our hats, shouted.*

33

FINGERS OF THE KOLOB

Unheralded Zion View

What a huge difference 0.4 of a mile can make.

Many Utahns have probably driven the five-mile Kolob Canyons scenic drive, just east of I-15, in a section of Zion National Park at exit 40. That's a signed turnoff and well-publicized. However, did you know that less than a half-a-mile drive off I-15 west at exit 42 yields an incredible but less heralded view of the Five Fingers of the Kolob—also part of the Kolobs Canyon section of Zion National Park?

In the New Harmony area, west of I-15, are amazing views of the Kolob, not visible from the freeway, which is too far east to allow such perspectives.

"One of the main attractions of New Harmony, and something it's famous for, is the Kolob Canyon Scenic Drive," Juli Danis, a southern Utah realtor, says on her website, www.julidanis.com. "If you drive into the town of New Harmony, and turn around and look towards the mountains on the east, you can see the magnificent view of the Kolob Fingers, truly one of the most magnificent sites you'll ever see. This is a well-kept secret, as traveling down the I-15 freeway, they are not visible to the routine traveler," she says.

The earliest mention of the view in newspapers was reported in the *Salt Lake Tribune* of September 5, 1960. Included in a writer's column of Views Remembered as Summer Fades was a mention of the "Kolob Terrace," glimpsed as one drives east on U-144 from New Harmony.

Less than two years later, the *Millard County Chronicle* in Delta, Utah, observed: "One interesting thing to look for on Interstate Highway 15,

The Fingers of the Kolob rise in northwestern Zion National Park. This view of the Fingers was taken about one mile west of I-15. *Courtesy of Liz Arave Hafen.*

near the little town of New Harmony, is the famous Kolob Fingers of Zion Canyon, formed by the tributaries of the Virgin River which carved Zion."

The late Craig D. Holyoak, a former artist for the *Deseret News*, who had worked in law enforcement in southern Utah before going into newspaper work, often mentioned his great appreciation for the works of nature in that part of the state. Among his favorite treasures was the Fingers of the Kolob.

There are some power lines that can get in the way of a photograph, but for any traveler headed to or from St. George, Las Vegas or California, it is worth it to at least once take five to ten minutes and exit the freeway west at exit 42 to see the Fingers of the Kolob—and to enjoy a scenic panorama invisible from the busy freeway.

PART VI

MAN-MADE WONDERS

34

MOKI DUGWAY

"Chill Factor" Cliff Driving

What the upper Angels Landing Trail in Zion National Park is to hiking (for many: scariest and most unforgettable), the Moki Dugway is to highway driving in Utah.

Sometimes referred to in Utah's San Juan County as "white knuckle hill," this three-mile-long unpaved road with an 11 percent grade is unique in the state highway system, for it is a segment of Utah Highway 261, from Mexican Hat to Highway 95 (south of Bear's Ears National Monument). For some, it is a shortcut to Hite Crossing on Lake Powell.

The road's switchbacks climb 1,200 feet up (or descend 1,200 feet down, as the case may be) a sandstone cliff face—and it has no guardrails. The dugway—an excavated road, usually on a hillside—is so camouflaged, blending into the colorful cliffs, that you have to almost be on the switchbacks to see them. At one point, the road drops 750 feet in just 440 yards.

"Going up or down is an experience not soon forgotten," is how the *San Juan Record* described driving the Moki Dugway on July 24, 1985. The dugway has become one of the area's attractions—and the nearby Muley Point Overlook doubles the eye candy.

Supposedly, the location of the Moki Dugway slope is where Ute chief Posey, though wounded, somehow came down the steep mountain in the 1920s and eluded lawmen intent on capturing him during what is considered the final Ute uprising. Posey apparently died in the desert of blood poisoning, ending the brief revolt.

The southeastern approach to the cliff-hugging and almost invisible Moki Dugway. Although it is a gravel road, the switchback is actually a segment of Utah Highway 261. *Ray Boren photo.*

According to the *San Juan Record* of July 13, 2005, the dugway's original name was Isabelle Hill, though no one seems to know why or when it switched to Moki. Why some variations of the name spell it "Moqui" or "Mokee" is also unknown, but the shortest spelling is generally the norm now, by common usage. The word is an old reference to Native Americans of the Four Corners area.

At the bottom, the Moki Dugway switchbacks begin at an elevation of 5,325 feet above sea level and top out at 6,525 feet on southeastern Utah's Cedar Mesa.

The *San Juan Record* of July 1, 1998, proclaimed that the road "gives new thrills to the driving experiences of the southwest" and "provides access to an overlook on top that provides panoramic views of the area."

How did this dugway come to be?

In 1955, The Texas Zinc Corp. began to build the dugway and a total of thirty-three miles of road from what is today's Utah Highway 95, south across Cedar Mesa to Mexican Hat, according to the *San Juan Record* of January 7, 1965. Plagued by strikes, the road was finally completed in mid-1957, providing direct access from the high elevation mines down to a uranium mill at Mexican Hat, near the Utah-Arizona border.

The dugway portion of the road alone cost $1 million (more than $9 million in 2020).

The road was deeded over to the State of Utah in 1957 and officially opened as a state highway on August 10, 1957. Even other portions of Highway 261 were not paved until 1961–62.

Texas Zinc Corp. was bought by Atlas Corp. in 1963, and the uranium mill at Mexican Hat closed in 1965.

San Juan County asked the Utah Department of Transportation to pave the road several times over the decades, including in 1971, according to the *San Juan Record* on January 21, 1971. However, that never happened, and the state road remains gravel today.

Because of the road's reputation, or their fears, some motorists choose to avoid the Moki Dugway entirely. To bypass it from below, travelers have to continue along US 191 from Mexican Hat toward Blanding, turning left onto U-95 toward Hite. The difference in distance is thirty extra miles without the dugway, or about thirty-seven minutes extra in travel time. If unaware of the dugway, it is likely motor home operators, big rig drivers and those afraid of heights who will question their sanity when they encounter the switchbacks traversing up or down.

The Moki Dugway drew Hollywood's attention when it was used as a setting in the 1999 thriller *Chill Factor*, starring Cuba Gooding Jr. and Skeet Ulrich.

Monument Valley High School held the Moki Dugway Hill Climb, a three-mile footrace, on December 14, 1991. Newspapers only contain one single reference to the race being held.

One Google review of the Moki Dugway describes it as an "incredibly scary gravel road…like going down the side of the Grand Canyon." Another recommends that only those unafraid of heights drive it, while others thought its "dangers" to be overrated.

The drop-off from Cedar Mesa has drawn other proposals. "Skyway Prospects Delight San Juan" was a December 29, 1968 headline in the *Salt Lake Tribune*. Reporter Carl E. Hayden reported that there was a plan to build a "sky railway" from the top of the Moki Dugway at Muley Point to Mexican Hat.

The concept would have had paying customers shuttled from Mexican Hat and up the dugway—about sixteen miles—in buses to ride a gravity-impelled cable car about twelve miles straight back to Mexican Hat. This "would give tourists the breathtaking joy of ascending the Moki Dugway," according to the *Tribune*.

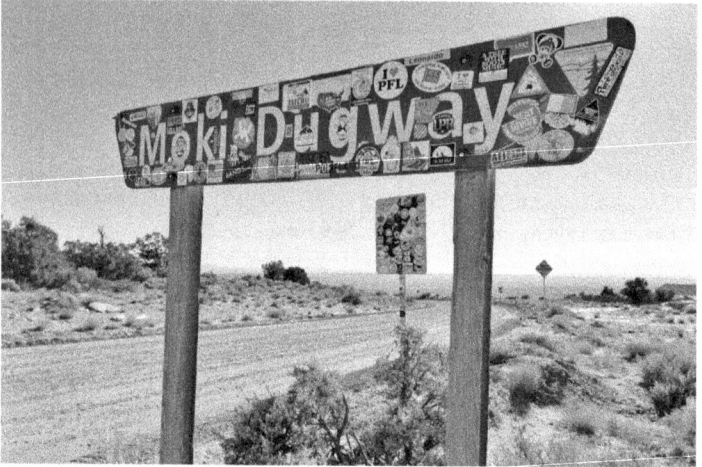

The Moki Dugway was completed in 1957. Its name origin is unknown but refers to ancient Indians. The route's original name was Isabelle Hill. *Ray Boren photo.*

Of course, the skyway was never built, and today, with controversy over increased commercial access to the nearby Bear's Ears area, sacred to Native Americans, such a development would probably never get any traction.

As for the dangers of the cliff-side highway: Yes, people have died on the Moki Dugway.

According to the *San Juan Record* of May 17, 1989, the first death happened about 1965. A man driving down the dugway stopped and got out of his truck to urinate at the first turn from the stop. A passenger in the truck said he heard the driver say, "Oh my God!" from the rear of the vehicle, and he was gone. His lifeless body was found on the next ridge below.

The newspaper said that scene was nearly repeated in 1989, when Howard Kinlicheeny, age twenty-six, was in a pickup with friends and also stopped to relieve himself. He slipped off the road and fell forty feet. He suffered a severed spinal cord and a fracture on his femur.

The *San Juan Record* of May 11, 1994, carried the headline "Mother Dies in One-Car Accident." Jane Madison Navaho, twenty-one, of Tonalea, Arizona, died when the car in which she was a passenger went off the road near the top of the dugway. She was thrown out of the vehicle as it plunged sixty feet and rolled over her. Her husband, Dickie Navaho, was injured and had to be extricated from the vehicle. The driver, Mary Stephens of

Pasadena, California, was able to crawl out of the car. She was the only one wearing a seat belt. The Utah Highway Patrol said Stephens was driving too fast and lost control coming down the dugway's first curve.

According to the *San Juan Record* of April 13, 2005, a family was almost to the bottom of the switchbacks that year when above them boulders the size of houses came loose and fell on the ledges above. They escaped injury, but a parked road grader higher up the Moki Dugway was damaged by rockfall.

And then there's a tale from the *San Juan Record* of July 22, 1987. A column by Doris Valle recounted the story of a driver who walked away from a fiery crash on the Moki Dugway, apparently in the early 1960s. Richard Nielson was starting to drive down the cliff's switchbacks in a uranium ore truck. The truck's brakes failed and then so did the steering, causing the vehicle to go over the first cliff coming down the dugway. Flames erupted under the hood, and Nielson's foot was caught by crumpled metal inside the cab. The flames suddenly died down but started again—twice—with a few minutes in between. Nielson finally got his foot unstuck and, though shaken up, climbed back up the hill to the top of the dugway.

He "came up behind two other truckers who stood aghast, looking down at the smoldering wreckage below," Valle wrote. "They were ready to climb down to find Richard's body when he tapped one on the shoulder. 'What're waiting for?'" he asked. "'Let's get on down the road!'"

35

ZION TUNNEL

Drilled from the Middle

A mid the heavenly natural wonders of Zion National Park, it's easy
to overlook one of man's engineering marvels—the Zion–Mount
Carmel Tunnel. The impressive, cave-like shaft is Utah's, and the
National Park system's, longest underground roadway, as well as the nation's
fifth-longest land tunnel. The 1.1-mile passageway and adjoining highway
were dedicated on July 4, 1930.

The main tunnel, a couple of smaller tunnels and the highway were
three years in the making, at a cost of almost $1.5 million: $937,000 for the
connecting highway, and $503,000 for the tunnel itself—more than $22.5
million in 2020. The project greatly improved access between Zion, Bryce
and Grand Canyon National Parks. The tunnel cut the Zion-to-Bryce travel
time in half—from about 150 miles to 88 miles, a difference of 62 miles—
and Zion–Grand Canyon travel by one-third.

And the early twentieth-century tunnel is considered a remarkable
engineering feat, for among other accomplishments, drilling actually started
in the middle.

The passage was built through and above Pine Canyon to connect Zion
Canyon with high plateaus to the east. Indians, we're told, had steered
clear of Zion for centuries because of its dark, forbidding, often dead-end
slots. The Southern Paiute called Zion Canyon *Ioogoon*—or "arrow quiver,"
interpreted to mean "come out the way you come in," the Park Service
says. The tunnel provided a second access to the park and alleviated that
quandary of one entrance/one exit.

Zion National Park's Zion–Mount Carmel Tunnel—more than a mile long—and the route's secondary tunnels were dedicated on July 4, 1930. *Ray Boren photo.*

Zion became a national monument in 1909 (first as Mukuntuweap and then as Zion in 1918) and a full-fledged national park on November 19, 1919, so it took twenty-one years after gaining federal park status for the tunnel project to come along. The tunnels themselves were desirable because they minimized cutting switchbacks into the sandstone cliffs for a roadway.

Parunuweap Canyon, farther south and directly east of Rockville, was the first route studied for a possible highway tunnel. However, Pine Canyon was eventually selected.

According to a newspaper story in the *Iron County Record* of October 26, 1929, survey crews spent two years climbing the mountain and evaluating the best tunnel route.

There was no trail to the top of Pine Mountain, so it was not feasible to do the tunnel survey from above. Surveyors used a special triangulation method to determine the tunnel's path from a foot trail that was some two hundred feet below tunnel level. Although it was the first time this type of survey had been used, the length of the tunnel connections varied by only two inches when finished.

The tunnel contract was awarded to the Nevada Construction Co. of Fallon, Nevada, and work was done in a four-section process that began in

1927. A contractor's camp was established below, in Pine Creek Canyon. A cable tramway traveled 1,200 feet across and 400 feet up from the bottom of Pine Creek to the camp, perched on slopes above and inaccessible by vehicle.

A pilot tunnel was first drilled through the sandstone mountain and then enlarged with an Erie Air Shovel to create a shaft twenty-two-feet wide and sixteen-feet high. The shovel used compressed air, creating less pollution and smoke. By one report, ten large holes were made in the mountain, which were then connected to create the tunnel.

A scaffold was also used on the side of the mountain. Waste was hauled by narrow-gauge railcars and then dumped through one of the six gallery openings or windows. Erosion and revegetation have removed most traces of this dumping below.

In a natural-preservation effort, work crews were careful to avoid disturbing trees in the area with the blasting. In addition, masonry the same color as the surrounding rock was used in the tunnel work.

However, the half-million-dollar tunnel project also had a higher price: Two workers were killed in separate accidents. Johnny Morrison, a crew boss, died after inhaling dynamite fumes. Mac McClain was killed when a large rock slid off the switchbacks and pinned him against a power shovel.

Other workers were injured during construction. The *Salt Lake Telegram* of November 8, 1928, for example, reported that a premature dynamite explosion seriously injured one worker. The *Washington County News* of January 1, 1928, said minor injuries resulted when one worker was struck by a falling block of ice and when another man fell ten feet off a ledge.

Historians say it took 146 tons of dynamite to complete the main tunnel and another 35 tons to make the switchbacks that access it. After one blast hurled a 10-pound piece of sandstone into the camp dining hall, wary occupants began running outside to look around every time a dynamite charge went off.

Carbide lights to see by and compressed air to blow away fumes were initially used in the tunnel. By 1928, electric power allowed crews to bring in electric lights and fans. In all, it took eleven months and twelve days to tunnel through the mountain.

The six switchbacks in Pine Creek Canyon that led up the tunnel from the west are 3.5 miles long and climb 800 feet, with a maximum grade of 6 percent.

The tunnel is not level. It climbs 289 feet (at a 3.3 percent grade) from the west to the east end. The west end of the tunnel is 4,835 feet above sea level, and the east end is at 5,124 feet. The Pine Creek Canyon switchbacks

A galley window in north side of the Zion Tunnel. The openings were drilled first to provide better access to and disposal of the rock, as well as ventilation. *Lynn Arave photo.*

begin at 4,000 feet above sea level, and the east entrance to Zion is 1,700 feet higher.

The Park Service built 8.5 miles of road inside the Zion Park boundaries to connect to the tunnel. In addition, the State of Utah spent $500,000 for its 16.5-mile road leading from Mount Carmel Junction and US 89 on the east to the park boundary.

The tunnel and roadway—State Highway 9—were dedicated in conjunction with the twenty-second annual National Conference of Governors that Utah hosted in 1930. The ceremony, on Independence Day, was held inside the tunnel, with the galleries decorated with U.S. flags. Salt Lake City's KSL Radio broadcasted a live report from the ceremony. B.J. Finch, district engineer for the U.S. Bureau of Public Roads, and Horace M. Albright, superintendent of the National Park Service, attended the dedication.

Finch said nature had determined millions of years ago where the tunnel would be and noted that it completed a new north–south route through Utah that people could enjoy. He praised the states of Utah and Arizona and the Park Service for their cooperation on the project.

Even though it is almost a century old, the Zion tunnel has not changed much over the years. Reinforcement work has been done because of the soft sandstone through which it was blasted, drilled and cut, the Park Service notes. Concrete ribs were added for support. Because of the potential for interior collapses, the tunnel is monitored electronically around the clock. And because some oversized vehicles use it, such as buses, motor homes and trailers, rangers are posted at both ends to temporarily stop two-way traffic and permit one-way access. Times are restricted and fees charged for such passage.

The Zion–Mount Carmel Tunnel was an engineering triumph—and the longest nonurban tunnel in the nation when it opened. In fact, Utah governor George H. Dern thought the tunnel such a marvel that he proposed that it be declared a separate national monument, according to the *Salt Lake Telegram* of December 30, 1929. He also suggested that the road around and through the tunnel be named the Stephen T. Mather Highway, in honor of the influential former director of America's national parks.

The governor's notions didn't make any headway, though.

36

U-143

Steepest State Road in Utah

What is deemed the steepest state highway in Utah—U-143 from the Parowan Valley to Cedar Breaks National Monument—was built up and onto the scenic Markagunt Plateau during the Great Depression, mainly in 1933–34.

According to the *Garfield County News* of August 10, 1934, the road was fully open by that date, much of it completed as part of a Civilian Conservation Corps (CCC) Camp effort.

The road has a 13 percent maximum grade and tops out at 10,567 feet above sea level. By comparison, most interstate highways only have a 6 percent maximum grade. The winding south central Utah road provides a challenging workout for any vehicle's brakes and engines.

The *Garfield County News* reported on August 25, 1933, that the route was originally known as the "Bowerly Road" and that part of its importance was connecting with the Duck Creek–Cedar Mountain Road—today's Utah Highway 14.

The newspaper outlined some of the challenges that builders faced when constructing the steep, eighteen-mile-long mountain route. One of them was to slice an eighty-foot-deep by one-thousand-foot-long cut through solid rock.

Final work on the adjacent Highway 14, from Cedar City past Navajo Lake and on to Long Valley Junction on US 89 north of Panguitch, was also done in the early 1930s, with most of that project being completed by the fall of 1932, according to the *Garfield County News* of September 2, 1932.

Highway 143 is considered the steepest paved state road in Utah, with a 13 percent grade. It was built in 1933–34 and tops out at 10,567 feet above sea level. *Lynn Arave photo.*

Such road construction provided much-needed employment to area men, many of whom were jobless or underemployed during the Great Depression. In fact, the U.S. Forest Service hired men for just two weeks at a time during 1932 so that other workers could also gain temporary employment for two weeks at a time.

Highways 143 and 14 both cross the Markagunt Plateau, roughly east to west and vice versa, through Dixie National Forest. A large swath of the area was ravaged by the seventy-two-thousand-acre Brian Head forest fire in 2017.

Cedar Breaks National Monument—established by President Franklin D. Roosevelt in the same era—on August 22, 1933—is poised between the two state highways above Cedar City, with short Highway 148 linking the park to both routes (except in winter, when U-148 is closed).

Cedar Breaks is an erosion-carved, cliff- and hoodoo-filled amphitheater. The landscape is similar to more-famous Bryce Canyon National Park, which is on the east end of the Paunsagunt Plateau, about sixty miles away.

37

DUCHESNE TUNNEL

Through the Uintas

W hen driving along Utah's Mirror Lake Highway (U-150), it is difficult not to constantly look upward and outward at the majestic peaks, slopes and canyons of the Uinta Range. However, below and just off the highway is a feature most travelers miss—the Duchesne Tunnel.

The tunnel is a six-mile-long engineering feat that is a key to providing water to Utah and Salt Lake Counties. The tunnel transports water from the south slope of the Uinta Mountains, in the Duchesne River drainage, and moves it over—and through—the mountains to the Provo River drainage toward Deer Creek Reservoir for storage.

Essentially, based on water rights, the tunnel conveys water initially destined for the Colorado River and the Pacific Ocean to the Provo River and the Great Basin's Great Salt Lake, which has no outlet to an ocean. Though, of course, the actual destiny of that water is to irrigate fields, quench urban thirsts and boost Utah's economy.

The outlet of the $9 million tunnel can be viewed above the Provo River at a stop along the Mirror Lake Highway in summer. The stop is signed on both the east and west ends of the highway. The west sign, however, is so close to the paved turnout that motorists might easily pass by and have to turn around and return. Watch for it 0.7 miles after Milepost 17, right after the Shady Dell Campground, on the right (south) side of the road for eastbound travelers.

The Duchesne Tunnel, six miles long, is a relatively hidden man-made treasure along Utah Highway 150 in the Uinta Mountains. *Lynn Arave photo.*

Although trees now obscure a good view of the portal, a one-hundred-foot-long path leads about forty feet down to a fenced viewpoint. There are also several historical plaques and informational placards there.

The tunnel required thirteen and a half years to build in the 1940s and 1950s. Delays slowed progress and included strikes by workers, World War II and Korean War manpower and financial shortages and a destructive fire.

One of the first references to the tunnel's construction was in the *Salt Lake Tribune* of May 4, 1941. "Work on the Duchesne tunnel also is proceeding rapidly," the story said, explaining that ninety men working three different shifts had hollowed out two thousand feet of tunnel during the first year of work.

World War II temporarily halted work on the tunnel. Yet, a *Salt Lake Telegram* story of December 30, 1941, argued that the project "is needed to supply additional water for defense developments in Salt Lake and Utah counties."

Less than a year later, work on the project was at a standstill when a fire destroyed a $100,000 power plant. Machinery and generators were ruined, and replacements had to come from San Francisco, according to the *Telegram* of October 20, 1942.

Next came the wartime hiatus. The *Provo Daily Herald* of January 7, 1946, observed that restrictions had finally come to an end, and tunnel work would resume soon.

Then, the *Daily Herald* of June 12, 1946, reported a new problem for the project: a concrete lining in the tunnel was now deemed necessary, raising the cost of the project by at least $900,000. Besides having another four miles left to dig, the lining meant considerable additional work.

The *Herald* of May 4, 1947, informed readers that the Bureau of Reclamation was going to have to call for new bids to finish the remaining 3.7 miles of the tunnel. The *Herald* followed on July 3, 1947, with the headline "Duchesne Tunnel encounters year delay because of bid rejections, but water shortage is not an immediate danger." The lowest bid received—$2.54 million—was one-third higher than the engineer's estimate.

An agreement was reached, and construction restarted, then almost three years later, in 1951, there was a major strike over job safety. The *Salt Lake Telegram* of March 21, 1951, said that workers claimed "hazardous working conditions" and "unreasonable demands for speed."

Work eventually restarted, but almost six months later, in October 1951, there were still some three thousand feet to go in the tunnel boring. The tunnel was extensively inspected, and it was estimated that it could be ready for use in 1952.

That estimate was wrong, because the Korean War in 1951 also halted construction.

The *Daily Herald* of December 6, 1951, reported that the tunnel was a mere 217 feet short of being "holed through." However, it was still going to have to be lined with cement, so the completion date was being reset for early 1953.

Workers were getting anxious for completion of the project, and they all contributed one dollar toward a pool to guess when the tunnel bore would be completed.

Tragedy struck in the tunnel project on July 24, 1952, when a worker was killed on the job. Stanley M. Elder, nineteen, was killed when he slipped into a sand chute and was buried under four feet of earth. The Heber City–based *Wasatch Wave* reported in a newspaper story on July 25 that workers saw a hand protruding from the sand and summoned help. The young man was removed within five minutes but could not be revived.

Workers celebrate the final breakthrough in the six-mile-long Duchesne Tunnel on December 12, 1951. Water was flowing through the tunnel by 1953. *Utah State Historical Society.*

The *Ogden Standard-Examiner* of August 4, 1952, carried the headline "Crews Working 3 Shifts a Day to Complete Duchesne Tunnel." Work on lining the tunnel walls with cement had begun on June 23. "Workers are now about one-quarter of the way into the giant tunnel and will soon be moving at a 300-foot per day clip," the newspaper said.

The *Salt Lake Tribune* of November 24, 1952, reported that cleanup work was all that remained on what was the longest tunnel ever bored in Utah. However, ample water supplies were expected to delay its use. The last concrete in the tunnel had been poured on November 10.

Finally, the *Ogden Standard-Examiner* reported on October 14, 1953, that the "6-mile Duchesne tunnel is done." Water that day was turned into the tunnel from the North Fork of the Duchesne River, erasing any concerns that the Salt Lake Valley would run out of water anytime soon. The system, part of the Provo River Project, was fully operational in 1954, according to the Provo River Water Users Association, which manages and maintains the tunnel and its equipment.

A special dam, the Duchesne Diversion, built in 1952 about twenty-one miles east of Kamas, supplies water for the tunnel. A control gate manages the flow into the tunnel.

The horseshoe-shaped, concrete-lined tunnel is ten feet in diameter and goes right through the rock core of the Uinta Mountains. Engineers of the era used slide rules and nonelectronic equipment to design it. One drilling team started on the east end (the inlet or east portal), on the North Fork of the Duchesne, and another on the west side (the outlet or west portal), on the Provo River—intending to meet in the middle.

When the two tunnels joined to become one, they were only a few inches off from each other—an engineering accomplishment of amazing accuracy.

38

GRANITE VAULTS

Arsenal of Genealogy

T he Granite Mountain Records Facility in Little Cottonwood Canyon
contains what is likely the world's most extensive collection of family
records.

Operated by the Church of Jesus Christ of Latter-day Saints, the vaults
are encased by the mountain, located about twenty miles southeast of Salt
Lake City. When these vaults, about one mile up the canyon, first opened in
1963, the public was invited for tours. However, by the end of the twentieth
century, the vaults were off limits to all but vault workers.

"LDS Buys Quarry Tract as Records Repository" was the September 29,
1959 headline in the *Salt Lake Tribune*. The story announced that the Utah
Granite Co. and Temple Granite Quarries Corp. had sold the land needed
for the records vault to the church. Exact details of the transaction were
never made public.

"Church Cuts Vaults in Granite Quarry" was a January 12, 1961 headline
in the *Salt Lake Tribune*. The story reported that some eighty years after the
Latter-day Saint Church first began chipping and hauling away granite
blocks for its future Salt Lake Temple, it was back in the same canyon doing
other work with the dominant stone there.

The Centennial Development Co. of Juab County had the contract to do
the excavation in the canyon. The company first drilled a seven-hundred-
foot exploration tunnel, which was to be followed by larger tunnels.

President Henry D. Moyle, second counselor in the church's First
Presidency, told Malin Foster of the *Tribune* that the vaults were being built

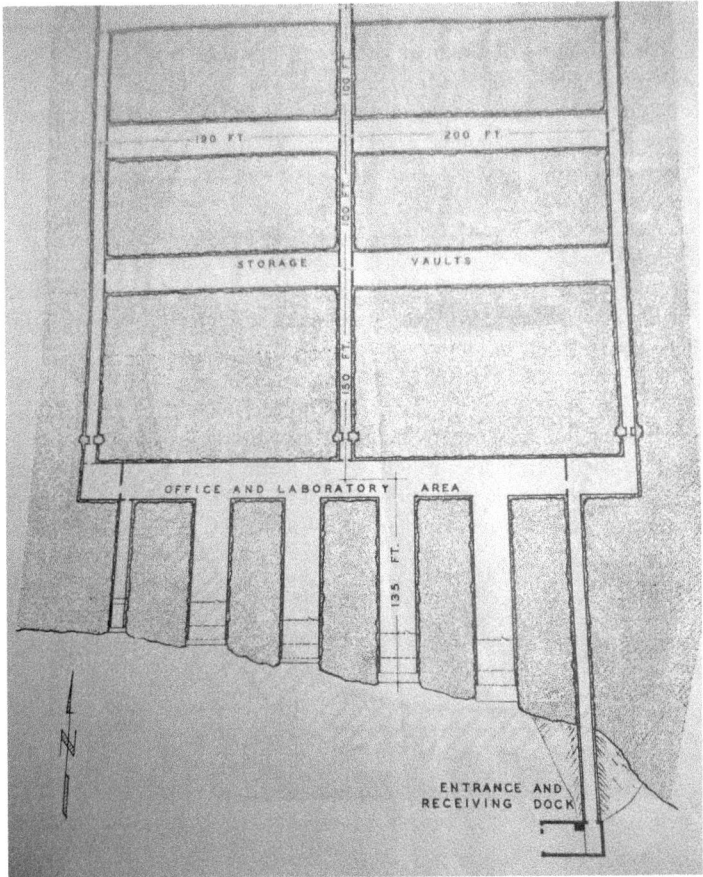

A drawing of the interior design of the Granite Records Vault in Little Cottonwood Canyon. *From promotional materials, the Church of Jesus Christ of Latter-day Saints.*

at the safest known place from disasters in the area for storing records. The rock vaults were also considered an ideal location for the storage of records based on temperatures and humidity.

"Drills Deepen Sanctuary for Church Records" was a May 29, 1961 headline in the *Tribune*. Staff writer Don LeFevre reported that a crew of fourteen men was cutting through the mountain's granite to create large caverns. "Their environment is a dark, damp and cool one as they labor on the construction of the vault which will one day house millions of dollars worth of valuable microfilm and documents," LeFevre wrote.

To that date, the drilling was through some 1,800 linear feet of rock, and completed channels measured 27 feet wide and 16 feet high. Six portals had been drilled into the mountain on the north side of the canyon, above Utah Highway 210.

The Little Cottonwood Canyon road leads to Snowbird and Alta ski resorts. A historic trail just inside the mouth of the canyon, on the south side and west of the vault site, marks and commemorates the quarry from which nineteenth-century workers cut granite blocks used to construct the Salt Lake Temple in downtown Salt Lake City.

"Crews Work in LDS 'Cave' Project" was a January 27, 1962 *Tribune* headline. By early 1962, crews were done drilling and were pouring cement and deciding the best type of flooring, walls and ceiling for this "cave." Trenches had been made in the floor for future plumbing and electrical lines. The story also noted that the church's First Presidency—the highest leadership—had chosen the site for records repository.

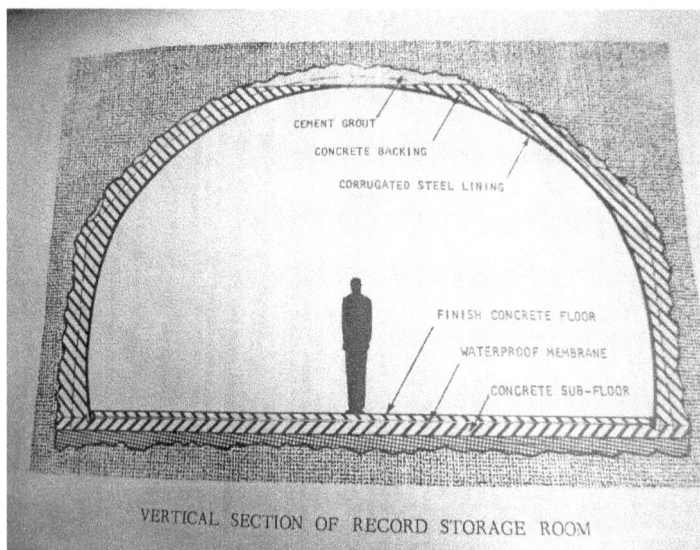

A sketch of the Granite Records Vault, showing its steel and concrete reinforcement. *From promotional materials, the Church of Jesus Christ of Latter-day Saints.*

Man-Made Wonders

"Impregnable Storage Vaults Safeguard LDS Genealogical Records" was an October 6, 1963 headline in the *Ogden Standard-Examiner*, above an Associated Press story. The report said the vaults were originally called the "Little Cottonwood Project" and had cost more than $1.5 million. It said the project had been more than three years in the making and was slated for completion in about one year.

The new repository would include three six-hundred-foot-long storage vaults lined with eighteen inches of cement and corrugated steel. Three large, heavy bank-like vault doors covered the entrances. The three main passages were also intersected by three others, more than four hundred feet long and all interconnected.

"LDS Grants Look-See of Tunnels" was a December 2, 1963 headline in the *Salt Lake Tribune*. Church leaders first toured the new granite vaults. Then selected civic and business leaders had their turn on day two, and finally, on the third day, the general public had a chance to take a look on guided tours. The facility was called simply the Church Records Vault when it opened. Today it is the Granite Mountain Records Facility.

The 1963 *Tribune* story said the insides of the vaults, "buried beneath 600 feet of solid granite," were painted in pastel colors, and the facility boasted self-contained power, water and ventilation.

There have been no public updates by the church about these fascinating record vaults. Presumably, they have been updated over the past half century and likely contain not only original microfilm records but also other forms of records storage, including CDs and other high-tech equipment.

Similarly, the U.S. Air Force had begun work on its own Cheyenne Mountain Complex in 1957, inside a granite mountain in Colorado, near Colorado Springs. That much larger vault was not completed until 1967, cost more than $142 million and sits underneath an estimated 2,000 feet of granite.

The *Salt Lake Tribune* of August 23, 1967, reported that landowners in Little Cottonwood Canyon had dropped a plan to build a housing subdivision at the mouth of the canyon in favor of constructing a private facility for microfilm and other storage inside the mountain itself. Located just up the canyon from the church's granite vaults, they were designed to be similar to those man-made caverns. Today, that facility is called Perpetual Storage Inc., located at 6279 Little Cottonwood Road.

39

KENNECOTT MINE

The Missing Mountain

Moving a mountain would seem, according to legend and practical imagination, one of the hardest things to do. After all, mountains are immovable, fixed in place—the ultimate in steadfastness. Right? Apparently, with patience and hard work, such a thing is possible, for a real mountain—a chunk of the Oquirrh Mountains on the west side of the Salt Lake Valley—is missing. A gaping hole remains.

It is the site of Rio Tinto Kennecott's Bingham Canyon open pit mine, where copper has been extracted for well over a century, creating in the process the world's largest man-made excavation. The Kennecott open-pit copper mine—considered the deepest in the world—is Utah's most impressive man-made feature. It was once described as one of only two such objects on the planet that can be spotted with the naked eye by orbiting astronauts. (The Great Wall of China is the other, though researchers say conditions would have to be just right.) At two and a half miles across and almost one mile deep, you could stack two Willis Towers (formerly and still better known as the Sears Tower) on top of each other and still not reach the top of the mine.

Most people today probably don't even realize that a mountain is missing at Bingham Canyon.

"It was a mountain," said Philip F. Notarianni, former director for the Utah State Historical Society and a lifelong resident of Magna, a community beside the northern tip of the Oquirrh Range.

Indeed, two large paintings in the Governor's Board Room in the Utah State Capitol depict clearly what early mining looked like in Bingham

Rio Tinto Kennecott's Bingham Canyon open pit mine is about two and a half miles across and nearly a mile deep. Salt Lake City is in the distance. *Ray Boren photo.*

Canyon, about twenty miles southwest of downtown Salt Lake City. In the early 1900s, the reverse of what we see now was true—a road spiraled upward as the copper mining process slowly chipped away at the mountain, before the "pit" came to be.

According to Lila Abersold, former visual arts manager for the Utah Arts Council, artist "Harry" H.L.J. Culmer created the capitol's two paintings of Bingham Canyon, probably sometime between 1910 and 1920, though no exact date has been verified. They were among the earliest paintings in the capitol collection and capture Culmer's fascination with the mining industry. "They are important paintings," Abersold said. "They offer a very early view of Bingham Canyon."

More than nineteen million tons of copper have been mined there—more than any other mine in history—as well as gold, silver and other metals. And the hole is just getting deeper. Rio Tinto keeps extending its plans and investments to continue digging and indicated that it intends to keep doing so at least until 2032, pending further extensions.

And even massive holes in the earth can change. A gigantic slide inside the Kennecott Mine in early 2013 changed the interior face of the mine. Even the visitor center had to be relocated after the event.

Slopes of Rio Tinto Kennecott's Bingham Canyon Mine, as seen from the southwestern Salt Lake Valley, where farming holds on even as suburbs approach. *Ray Boren photo.*

In Bingham Canyon's early days (1863–1900), all mining was done underground, as tunnels were dug into the mountain. Miners were also then looking for gold, silver or lead, because the forty pounds of copper per ton of ore wasn't a profitable process then. By the late 1890s, all the easy mining had been done, and new concepts were being considered for the district.

Engineers Daniel Jackling and Robert Gemmell surveyed Bingham Canyon and suggested that low-grade porphyry copper ore could profitably be mined from the surface on a larger scale, using railroad cars and steam shovels. Their first report showed that the cost of producing one pound of refined copper would be six cents. With the selling price of copper at fourteen to eighteen cents a pound, their report looked impressive on paper.

There were skeptics, but by August 1906, steam shovels mounted on railroad tracks began digging into the mountain.

Less than three years later, the Utah Copper Co. had 11 steam shovels, 21 locomotives, 145 dump cars and 16 miles of railroad tracks on the mountain. After buying out the Boston Consolidated Mining Co., which owned a portion of the mountain, mining really took off.

The "hill," as it was called, got smaller and smaller, and in 1912, there were five thousand mine workers.

A major improvement came in the 1920s, when electricity replaced steam to power the shovels and locomotives. Shovels were also mounted on caterpillar tractors, giving workers more freedom to move about.

In fact, the *Deseret News* in December 1922 reported that "a mountain once more begins to move" as mining activity increased dramatically at Bingham Canyon. "A whole mountain of copper is actually being moved away," the *News* reported.

By the 1930s, the "hill" was gone, and a pit began to develop. In 1936, Kennecott Copper Corp., which previously had a partial investment in the enterprise, bought out the Utah Copper Co. After a few other exchanges over the decades, the international Rio Tinto Group acquired the Bingham Canyon Mine and its mill and smelter facilities in 1989.

40

KENNECOTT SMOKESTACK

Reaching for the Sky

Kennecott Copper's towering smelter smokestack scrapes the sky west of Salt Lake City, at the northern tip of the Oquirrh Mountains and just off the south shore of the Great Salt Lake. Although it is one of the loftiest free-standing structures in the world—and the tallest such thing west of the Mississippi in the United States—it is rarely recognized as such, making it one the unheralded manmade icons in Utah.

Rising abruptly about a dozen miles west of Salt Lake City and just south of I-80, the Garfield Smelter Stack, constructed in 1974, is by far the tallest man-made structure in Utah at 1,215 feet. It is just a tad shorter than New York City's 102-story Empire State Building (1,250 feet high, excluding its antenna) or, in Utah terms, equal to the height of three LDS Church Office Buildings. The smokestack's hexagon-shaped base is an impressive 177 feet across.

Indeed, the *Ogden Standard-Examiner* newspaper of November 28, 1974, carried the headline "Kennecott Smokestack 50 Feet Short of Empire State Building" (though it is actually even less than that). In a previous story, on March 19, 1974, the *Standard-Examiner* had reported that the smokestack, when completed, would be the second-highest exhaust stack on the American continents.

If a six-foot-two-inch-tall person were standing next to the tallest of NBA basketball players, they would probably seem pretty short. In similar fashion, Kennecott Copper's Garfield Smelter smokestack is dwarfed as it stands adjacent to the nine-thousand-plus-foot Oquirrh Mountains, which rise more than four thousand feet above the Salt Lake Valley.

The Garfield smokestack, part of the Rio Tinto Kennecott mining operation, rises 1,215 feet above the Salt Lake Valley beside the Oquirrh Mountains. *Ray Boren photo.*

A look inside its base reveals a surprising amount of open space, surrounded by concrete up to 12 feet thick. The concrete structure itself towers to an even 1,200 feet, and a fiberglass flue continues upward another 15 feet.

"It's overkill for this [refinery] plant," according to Jack Haymond, a consulting engineer for Kennecott. "But it was here....It would cost a fortune to take it down." He said Kennecott built the stack after the federal Clean Air Act came along in 1970. At the time, it was a good fit. It was just high enough to disperse waste gases, according to the new standards. However, with leaping advances in pollution controls since, it is now taller than it needs to be.

Haymond said Kennecott, owned by Rio Tinto, is one of the two cleanest smelters in the world, capturing 99.9 percent of all the sulfur gas released.

The chimney replaced several predecessor Kennecott smokestacks, now demolished, the tallest of which had a height of 413 feet.

"They commandeered every cement truck in northern Utah" when they built it in 1974, Haymond said. Concrete flowed—more than twenty-six thousand cubic yards—for eighty-four days, twenty-four seven, minus one short break, to complete it. Some nine hundred tons of steel were also required.

Completed in 1974, the Garfield smokestack is almost the height of the Empire State Building. *Lynn Arave photo.*

Work on the stack began on August 26, 1974, and was finished in less than three months. It cost $16.3 million to build, the equivalent of more than $70 million in early twenty-first-century dollar values.

The stack was built according to Zone 3 seismic standards, the company said. And it has been rattled by earthquakes. A series of temblors in the spring of 2020, for example, shook Utah's Magna area and beyond, including the Garfield structure. A chemical leak was reported at the refinery, but there was no major structural damage.

What about lightning? Haymond said he's only aware of one instance when nature jolted the smokestack from the sky. He said in the mid-1980s, he came to work one day during a maintenance shutdown period and found pieces of concrete on the roadway below the stack. Lightning had chipped the top. It was soon repaired, but "no one saw the strike," he said.

Jana Kettering, a Kennecott spokeswoman, said the stack is an icon for people traveling in and out of the Salt Lake Valley. Boaters she knows, who sail the Great Salt Lake, use it as a key geographical indicator. Airline pilots and frequent flyers also have been known to use it as a landmark. And it can be spotted from as far away as portions of Box Elder County, across the Great Salt Lake.

Strobe lights at two intensities—brighter in the day and not as bright at night—alert airplanes and helicopters to its proximity.

Although there is a two-person cage-type elevator inside the smokestack that travels to the top, it is rarely used. "It's a long, scary ride," Haymond said, and it takes about twenty minutes to reach the top. Today, a worker only needs to travel up to the three-hundred-foot level each day to service an air-sampling station.

The top of the smokestack narrows to forty feet in diameter and features twelve-inch-thick concrete.

The smokestack is also part of Kennecott's efficient smelter process, which supplies about 60 percent of its own electrical energy needs through steam generation.

A 1,765-foot-long piping system carries leftover gases into the smokestack, and an interior pipe travels inside the concrete and up to the top of the stack. Haymond said any discharge you see out of the smokestack isn't smoke; it is just steam. Only trace amounts of any waste gases escape.

According to a Wikipedia ranking of freestanding structures (those that lack guyed masts or support cables), the Kennecott Smokestack is the thirty-first-tallest structure (including skyscrapers) in the world. In the United States, it is ranked fifth highest, behind the Willis Tower (formerly Sears Tower) and the John Hancock Center, both in Chicago; the Empire State Building in New York City; and a smokestack a mere two feet taller in Pennsylvania.

In comparison, the Las Vegas Stratosphere is 66 feet shorter at 1,149 feet high. Seattle's Space Needle is just 605 feet tall, less than half the Utah smokestack's height.

The Kennecott smokestack, fourth tallest chimney in the world, is the only operating smelter chimney left in Utah. As a working facility with potential hazards about, public tours are not offered at the smokestack or refinery.

41

FRANCIS PEAK

Lofty Outpost of Domes

O nce one of the craggiest local summits, Francis Peak today is one of the most altered high points in the Wasatch Range. The mountain lost its pointy top when two radar domes were built there in the late 1950s.

Rising east of Fruit Heights and Farmington along the Wasatch Front and straddling the Davis County/Morgan County line, Francis Peak was also one of the first local mountain peaks to be named. It was dubbed "Francis" at the suggestion of pioneer leader Brigham Young, in honor of Esther C.E. Francis (1836–1913), who helped settle the Morgan area in 1860s.

Our Heritage: Samuel and Esther Francis describes it this way: "Rising majestically above Morgan Valley to the west of the Wasatch Mountains, one of its highest peaks bears the name 'Francis Peak.' Snowcapped and glittering in the sun in the day and lit by two artificial lights by night, it stands as a lighthouse in the sky to be seen for many miles."

With two man-made radar domes sitting atop Francis Peak today, it looks far different than it did before the late 1950s.

The domes, operated by the Federation Aviation Administration (FAA) and the Air National Guard, provide long-range radar and identification for aircraft. The facility's radar range is 250 miles outward and up to 100,000 feet straight up.

At first, the FAA wanted to install such a radar site near Alta or Snowbird, farther south. However, the National Guard was already using a temporary

Francis Peak is a lonely radar outpost in the Wasatch Mountains of Utah's Davis County. The FAA keeps the road to the summit open year-round. *Lynn Arave photo.*

facility atop Francis Peak, so that became the logical shared location. Otherwise, according to the *Salt Lake Tribune* of September 26, 1958, Francis Peak was only initially planned to host a National Guard installation. That story states that Francis Peak's original elevation was 9,547. After being leveled for the radar facility, and counting the artificial structure, the height dropped by 32 feet to 9,515.

Workers atop Francis Peak had to wear thick, high boots and carry weapons. Rattlesnakes are not supposed to live that high, yet someone forgot to tell the rattlers that. Numerous rattlesnake nests were uncovered during construction, despite the almost two-mile-high altitude.

In fact, according to the *Standard-Examiner* of September 26, 1958, almost one hundred rattlesnakes had to be killed by workers during construction. A *Standard-Examiner* story from September 21, 1958, observed that rattlesnakes were exterminated at the rate of two or three a day during the construction process. Two workers were bitten. Both survived.

"Morgan County Sees New Stars (Radar Unit Lights) atop Peak" was the headline of the latter story. It also reported that sand and gravel trucks came from the Bountiful end of the Wasatch ridgeline, along Skyline Drive (not through Farmington Canyon) and that it took six hours for such trucks to make the trip.

Approximately twenty-two thousand cubic yards of material and nearly a dozen yards of the peak's height were removed to level the summit. The $2 million construction project, in 1958–59, also included helicopters flying in thirty-three gigantic metal poles, weighing eight hundred to one thousand pounds each, to shore up a foundation.

Francis Peak today is a lofty, high-tech outpost, complete with a kitchen, bedrooms and its own water supply. It is a twin, of sorts, to the TV and radio broadcast transmission facility on Farnsworth Peak in the Oquirrh Mountains to the southwest.

So how tall is Francis Peak?

The U.S. Geological Survey lists Francis Peak as 9,547 feet above sea level. However, that was *before* the 1950s construction. The modified height is now 9,515 feet. The radar facility's base adds 55 feet, and the radar domes chip in 60 feet more for a total extra artificial height of 115 feet and a grand total of 9,630 feet above sea level. Only Thurston Peak, about four miles north, is "taller" in Davis County, at 9,706 feet.

The Francis Peak radar domes have been "skymarks" along the Wasatch Front since the late 1950s. This is how they appear from Layton. *Lynn Arave photo.*

The FAA uses special rotary snow blowers to keep the unpaved road to the radio domes accessible year-round, since it is manned continually. However, a seventeen-thousand-foot-long tramway access was proposed to be constructed up Shepard Canyon in 1977. Environmental concerns delayed and eventually doomed that project.

The Civilian Conservation Corps (CCC) built the Farmington Canyon–Bountiful Peak road during from 1935 to 1939. The twenty-six-mile loop, officially known today as the Skyline Drive Scenic Backway, first opened to the public in July 1939. Steep grades, narrow curves and sheer drops still test the nerves of drivers venturing to the mountaintops.

Some fifty years of overgrazing by domestic sheep led to disastrous flash floods down the mountainside and into the communities below in both 1923 and 1930. The dirt road was originally built to aid access for the approximately eighty men of Bountiful CCC Camp No. 910 to construct flood-control terraces and seeding projects from Parrish Canyon on the south to Farmington Canyon on the north. After that, the road helped the U.S. Forest Service keep erosion and wildfires under control. The route's bonus was opening the scenic beauty of this section of the Wasatch to public access.

Workers and sheepherders also reported rattlesnakes at unusually high elevations there in the late 1930s.

When construction on the radar domes took place in the late 1950s, the FAA built the additional five-mile dirt road northward, from the top of Farmington Canyon to Francis Peak.

A Jeep trail continues north from the radar domes and eventually swings to the backside of the Wasatch Mountains to access the three Smith Creek Lakes on the Morgan side.

Francis Peak and Skyline Drive are popular summertime scenic backway destinations in Davis County, offering access to campgrounds, as well as the most spectacular bird's-eye views possible of the Great Salt Lake. The Sunset Campground, at an elevation of 6,200 feet in Farmington Canyon, opened in 1939 but was decommissioned in 2018. The Bountiful Peak Campground, tucked under the east side of the range at 7,500 feet, was dedicated in 1941.

Skyline Drive begins on its north end on Farmington's 100 East. It is paved for the first mile and then follows a winding, narrow dirt route up and down the high ridges. Most passenger cars can make this bumpy journey, though it is a backcountry road.

There is a fork in the road at the top of Farmington Canyon, about eight miles up. The right (south road) leads to Bountiful Peak and eventually

Bountiful's east bench, some nineteen miles later. The road on the left (north) is the one that heads to the FAA radar domes on Francis Peak. A gate on the left fork is closed during snow season because of dangerous snow removal equipment.

Snowbanks along the upper reaches of the road—at and above nine thousand feet in elevation—usually persist until mid- to late July. From the summits and on a clear day, even the High Uintas are visible to the east.

A popular ATV and hiking trail leads northeast from the radar towers to the Smith Creek Lakes.

Before 2002, people could drive or walk right up to Farmington Peak's radar domes. Now fencing and enhanced security better protect the facilities.

The Farmington Canyon road leading to the radar domes has a history of its own. According to the *Ogden Standard-Examiner* of September 1, 1937, the origin of the road dates to 1936. In its first two years of construction, 64 tons of dynamite, thirty-three thousand gallons of gasoline and 26,069 manhours were required to build the road—and that was just the first seven and a half miles up the mountain.

42

SPIRAL JETTY

Art with a Salty Twist

I f you Google search for "famous land art" or something similar, among the locations and artwork most likely to pop up first will be Robert Smithson's *Spiral Jetty*. It is, in its own way and genre, famous and will be at or near the top of any list of such creations.

A half-century ago, the (literally and figuratively) groundbreaking American artist designed and, equipped with bulldozers and muscular dump trucks, had a construction crew build what has become his most famous landscape "earthwork" off a northern beach of Utah's Great Salt Lake. The end result was completed in the spring of 1970 after a little rethinking on Smithson's part. The original resembled the letter *J*; he had his workers reshape it into a spiral, a form familiar in Native American pictographs and in nature, as with exotic ferns. Smithson's final version was a dark, multi-coiled levee constructed with about six thousand tons of black basalt rock. The boulders and stones, quarried in the same vicinity, curled 1,500 feet into (and in drier times, toward) the pink-to-purple shallows of Rozel Bay.

The spot, a trust-land parcel leased from the State of Utah, offered Smithson just what he envisioned for his rough masterwork: a stark landscape fit for a concept that he apparently hoped would reflect both timeless antiquity and long-term decay, or entropy. It had a briny lake, enhanced by reddish water, the latter an effect he was aware of elsewhere and which chroniclers say intrigued him. The pigments in the Great Salt Lake, researchers report, are due to tiny but multitudinous microbes like

An aerial view of artist Robert Smithson's *Spiral Jetty*, where it appears more a part of the lakescape than it does at ground level. The artwork is about fifty miles west of Brigham City. *Ray Boren photo.*

halophilic ("salt-loving") archaea, algae and bacteria, which thrive on occasion in the lake's extremely salty north arm.

Several other factors seem to play into *Spiral Jetty*'s allure.

For one thing, it is adventurously outback: one hundred miles from Salt Lake City at a desert site ultimately accessed by a washboard-textured gravel-and-dirt ranch road fifteen miles from pavement that ends at the already remote Golden Spike National Historic Park at Promontory Summit. That is where the Golden Spike was driven into the rails to complete the world's first Transcontinental Railroad in 1869.

Another factor is a tragedy. Robert Smithson died in 1973, only three years after he finished *Spiral Jetty*, at age thirty-five, in a small-plane crash while overseeing construction of another landscape artwork in Texas, his *Amarillo Ramp*. He is the dead-too-soon rock star of his art form.

And then there is the mercurial nature of the Great Salt Lake itself.

The inland sea tends to rise and fall dramatically. It is what geologists and hydrologists call an endorheic or terminal lake, one that lacks an outlet stream linking it to another body of water or ocean. The water in such lakes is usually salty and brackish. The elements don't have anywhere to go. The Great Salt Lake is generally about 75 miles long by 35 miles wide, according to the Utah Geological Survey, with an average surface elevation at 4,200 feet above sea level. Soon after *Spiral Jetty* was finished, even Smithson realized it was going to occasionally drown, for it was built at 4,197 feet. The fluctuating lake waters were rising after being at a historic low in 1963, when it had a surface elevation of 4,191.35 feet.

Spiral Jetty vanished for most of the next thirty-plus years. A vast amount of water poured into the Great Salt Lake basin during the wet mid-1980s, often called the "flood years" by Utahns who witnessed the aftermath, when northern Utah experienced above-average precipitation. The historic surface elevation, according to the Geological Survey, peaked at 4,211.85 feet from 1986 to 1987. The lake spread out. Bird refuges, industrial solar ponds, freeways, causeways and railways were damaged or endangered. *Spiral Jetty* disappeared. Afterward, the jetty reemerged a few times, notably in the early 1990s, or was visible simply as a shadow beneath the waves. By the early 2000s, as lake levels receded, it appeared that *Spiral Jetty* was about to rise again.

And it did. Bits of the tallest basalt boulders poked up in 2002. And in the summer of 2003, *Spiral Jetty* was reborn, emerging marinated, bright white and spackled with layers of salt. We've said it before: The jetty was so beautiful for a while that it probably would have surprised even Robert Smithson.

The encrustations did not last, for exposure melted the salts away. Occasionally, over the intervening years, a "wet year" with high precipitation along Great Salt Lake's tributaries will allow levels to rise again and briefly swamp *Spiral Jetty*. But in general Smithson's landscape artwork is found baking under a blazing sun, high and dry on the cracked and dusty lakebed, with the water's edge somewhere off in the near distance. Puddles sometimes accumulate in the jetty's coils or in nearby depressions.

For a few decades, *Spiral Jetty* was just about forgotten. But since 2003, it has been visited, photographed, filmed and written about far more than was the case before it resurfaced. Big tomes have been written about it. For example, the Dia Art Foundation, to which the earthwork was bequeathed by the artist's estate, published *Robert Smithson's Spiral Jetty* (2005), a compendium of pieces by Smithson himself and other writers about the work. Utah art historian Hikmet Sidney Loe compiled *The Spiral Encyclo* (2017), an encyclopedic array of articles, analyses, critiques and factoids.

In the wake of *Spiral Jetty*, landscape sculpture and related artifacts are not uncommon. Even Utah has other sites of interest.

Later in the 1970s, Smithson's wife, the late artist Nancy Holt, created a similarly remote attraction west of the Great Salt Lake, called *Sun Tunnel*—four huge concrete tubes, aligned in an *X* shape, frame the rising and setting sun on June's Summer Solstice and December's Winter Solstice.

Karl Momen's multi-storied *Metaphor: The Tree of Utah* rises spectrally beside Interstate 80 near the Bonneville Salt Flats east of the Utah-Nevada border, haunting motorists and tourists driving east or west for miles.

Andrew Rogers's *Ratio Utah*, a stack of giant white and black blocks, with a golden one at the tower's apex, is said to reflect the mathematical Fibonacci sequence. It sits beside Interstate 70 near Green River, Utah.

Other landscape artworks might be more scientifically curious (Walter De Maria's *The Lightning Field* in New Mexico); more ambitious (James Turrell's *Roden Crater*, a naked-eye observatory being created in a dormant Arizona volcano); more fanciful (Ugo Rondinone's *Seven Magic Mountains*, brightly painted stacked-boulder pillars outside of Las Vegas); or vaster (Michael Heizer's mysterious *City*, as of this writing still in progress north of Las Vegas).

Yet Utah's *Spiral Jetty* likely will remain a Google-worthy earthwork for aficionados, sightseers, art history books—and the ages.

BIBLIOGRAPHY

Part 1. Mysterious Places

Arave, Lynn. "Chinatown: Remote Geological Wonder of Morgan County." *Ogden Standard-Examiner*, April 30, 2015.
———. "Navajo Mountain Is Little-Known Giant." *Deseret News*, March 2, 2004.
———. "Peter Sinks: Utah's Coldest Spot." *Deseret News*, August 8, 1990.
———. "Picturesque Noah's Ark Floats amid a Sea of Beautiful Southern Utah Scenery." *Deseret News*, November 8, 2007.
Ray, Boren. "Utah's Rainbow Bridge: Between Heaven and Earth." *Deseret News*, February 12, 1998.
———. "'World's Longest Gallery' Takes Your Breath Away." *Deseret News*, March 5, 1998.

Part II. Legends of Utah's Past

Arave, Lynn. "An Actual Howard Stark—Not the Fictional Father Iron Man Tony Stark—and a Real Plane Crash in Utah." *Deseret News*, August 18, 2020.
———. "Ben Lomond: 'Mountain of Dreams.'" *Ogden Standard-Examiner*, June 6, 2014.

———. "Layton's Snow Horse Gallops into View on Mountainside." *Deseret News*, June 2, 1993.

———. "Old Ephraim: Utah's Most Legendary Bear." *Ogden Standard Examiner*, July 6, 2015.

———. "Utah Nearly Hosted the A-Bomb Project." *Deseret News*, February 9, 2009.

———. "When Hollywood Disliked Southern Utah's Brightly Colored Terrain—and Even Got Stranded." *Deseret News*, July 14, 2020.

Part III. Utah Highs and Lows

Arave, Lynn. "Explorer Thought La Sals' Snow Was Salt." *Deseret News*, November 19, 1999.

———. "Peak Is Eye-Catching. Summit Like a Beehive or a Pyramid." *Deseret News*, October 18, 2002.

———. "Utah's Basement—Beaver Dam Wash Is State's Lowest Elevation." *Deseret News*, September 3, 2006.

———. "When Kings Peak Wasn't Utah's 'Tallest.'" *Ogden Standard-Examiner*, July 24, 2014.

Arave, Lynn, and Ray Boren. "A Desert Discovered: Utah's House Mountains." *Deseret News*, August 24, 1997.

———. "Hiking Nebo: Named for a Biblical Mount Near the Dead Sea, Highest Peak of the Wasatch is an Adventure." *Deseret News*, September 11, 1994.

Part IV. Utah Heaven and Hell

Arave, Lynn. "Come to Zion: National Park Abounds in Religious References." *Deseret News*, May 23, 2010.

———. "Don't Judge Hiking by Strange Names of Peaks." *Deseret News*, July 7, 1994.

———. "Great Stone Face, Formation Resembles Prophet." *Deseret News*, May 13, 2010.

———. "The Mystery of Monte Cristo." *Deseret News*, June 21, 1996.

———. "Pioneers Had a Devil of a Time in Utah." *Deseret News*, December 17, 2002.

———. "What's the Story Behind Devil's Slide in Morgan County." *Ogden Standard-Examiner*, September 25, 2014.

Arave, Lynn, and Ray Boren. "Cathedral Valley—Capitol Reef's Spectacular Northern Badlands." *Deseret News*, November 23, 2003.

Part V. Forgotten Places

Arave, Lynn. "Fremont Island Is No Disappointment." *Deseret News*, April 16, 2009.

———. "Lagoon: It's Not Where It Used to Be." *Ogden Standard-Examiner*, August 29, 2016.

———. "Looking Back at Malan's Heights: 'Copacabana of the West.'" *Ogden Standard-Examiner*, June 11, 2015.

———. "This Is the Place Monument Isn't Quite at Actual 'Place.'" *Deseret News*, July 24, 2009.

Part VI. Man-Made Wonders

Arave, Lynn. "Driving U-143 Will Put Your Breaks to the Test." *Deseret News*, May 26, 2000.

———. "Francis Peak Offers Views, Hikes and Radar Domes." *Deseret News*, July 4, 1998.

———. "Holy Smokes: Kennecott Smelter, Utah's Tallest Man-Made Structure, to Turn 35." *Deseret News*, November 16, 2009.

———. "Rock on Through: Zion Tunnel Is an Engineering Marvel, an Environmental Model and an Aesthetic Delight." *Deseret News*, July 16, 1995.

———. "Utah Pit Was Once a Mountain." *Deseret News*, December 31, 2003.

NOTE: Most chapters are adapted and expanded stories from the originals. Also, some material is from Lynn Arave's blog, *The Mystery of Utah History*.

ABOUT THE AUTHORS

Lynn Arave graduated from Weber State University with degrees in communications-journalism and human performance. He worked for the *Deseret News* for thirty-two years, first as a sportswriter, then as a feature writer and finally as a City Desk reporter and editor. He has written six books. One is *Walking Salt Lake City* (2012, cowritten with Ray Boren) and another is *Images of America Layton Utah* (2020). He also maintains many blogs, including *The Mystery of Utah History*, used often by Utah fourth- and seventh-grade history classes. Lynn lives in Layton with his wife, LeAnn Flygare Arave. The couple have four children and three grandchildren.

Ray Boren, a lifelong Utahn, is a writer, editor and photographer. He graduated from the University of Utah with a degree in mass communications. He worked at the *Deseret News* for thirty-five years as a reporter, feature writer, editor and ultimately deputy managing editor. His current focus is on photography, freelance writing, book projects and travel. He cowrote *Walking Salt Lake City* with Arave and provided the photographs for the book. He lives in Salt Lake City.

Visit us at
www.historypress.com

www.ingramcontent.com/pod-product-compliance
Lightning Source LLC
Chambersburg PA
CBHW070330100426
42812CB00005B/1317